THEORY OF Sellativity

Turning Sales Theory Into Results.

By Jeff Lewis

COPYRIGHT

By Jeff Lewis

www.sellativitysolutions.com

All rights reserved.
Book Layout ©2015 EvolveInstantAuthor.com

No part of this book may be reproduced or transmitted in any form or by any means, electronic or mechanical, including photocopying, recording or by any information storage and retrieval system, without written permission from the authors, except for the inclusion of brief quotations in a review.

Limit of Liability Disclaimer: The information contained in this book is for information purposes only, and may not apply to your situation. The author, publisher, distributor and provider provide no warranty about the content or accuracy of content enclosed. Information provided is subjective. Keep this in mind when reviewing this guide. Neither the Publisher nor Authors shall be liable for any loss of profit or any other commercial damages resulting from use of this guide. All links are for information purposes only and are not warranted for content, accuracy, or any other implied or explicit purpose.

Earnings Disclaimer: All income examples in this book are just that – examples. They are not intended to represent or guarantee that everyone will achieve the same results. You understand that each individual's success will be determined by his or her desire, dedication, background, effort and motivation to work. There is no guarantee you will duplicate any of the results stated here. You recognize any business endeavors has inherent risk or loss of capital.

Theory Of Sellativity 1st Edition. 2015
ISBN-13: 978-1512325911
ISBN-10: 1512325910

Table of Contents

Foreword v
Endorsements vii
The Secrets of Sellativity Finally Revealed vii
Sellativity Makes Sales More Than Just a Numbers Game. ix
About Jeff Lewis xi
Introduction xxi

CHAPTER ONE 27
    The Story Behind the Story 27

CHAPTER TWO 37
    The Theory of Sellativity 37

CHAPTER THREE 53
    Preparation 53

CHAPTER FOUR 69
    Process 69

CHAPTER FIVE 87
    Getting a Decision 87

CHAPTER SIX 113
    Unconsciously Incompetent 113

CHAPTER SEVEN 119
    Selling Points 119

CHAPTER EIGHT 129
    Closing the Sale 129

CHAPTER NINE 153
    Closing Technique 153

CHAPTER TEN 177
    Overcoming Objections 177

CHAPTER ELEVEN 203
    Conclusion 203

Foreword

I owe a tremendous debt of gratitude to the selling of books. The experience of selling story books, children's books, educational and lesson teaching materials was the foundation of my success. It offered many and various opportunities to practice and "get it right".

It began with selling books door-to door in Midwest USA. A combination of sales managers, books, tapes, seminars, motivational events and most importantly, hands-on face-to-face experience with customers established the foundation of what has become my "Theory of Sellativity".

I also believe the training I received early on was responsible for setting the tone to make me realise that there was a lot to learn in order to excel in this profession.

There were many people who inspired me, and I thank them for helping me find my way and insisting that I learn the right way… however one very important individual deserves acknowledgment in acting as an absentee mentor; Zig Ziglar. His books, seminars, methods and sales presentation aids were instrumental in developing the understanding of the sales process for me.

Zig Ziglar unlocked the essence of what selling as a professional should be and that got me. Zig presented real life and common sense along with the "why" where others might be good at showing you what to do, the "why" to do it was the formula for me. I quote or refer to Zig often in this book, because lessons and memories are irreplaceable and many of them relate back to life experiences.

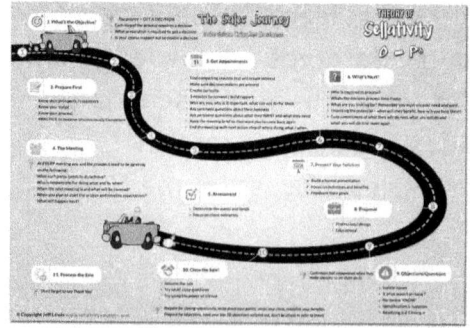

Get your beautiful FREE bonus
"Sales Journey Wall Chart"

Visit
www.sellativitysolutions.com

Endorsements

The Secrets of Sellativity Finally Revealed

> **Peter Whalley,**
> **Managing Director of Sybiz Software**

"It's fair to say that Jeff has been a wonderful influence, not only in my "sales" life, but in other areas too. Over a number of years of close observation of Jeff's professional (and dare I say enthusiastic) conversations with numerous customers, I have been lucky enough to walk away with some golden nuggets of sales wisdom, which I have used to great effect in my own customer interactions.

Many of these secrets are now available to you in "Theory of Sellativity." It's also fair to say that the very nature of a book will not be able to bring to life the reality and magic of Jeff's ability to quickly and emphatically lower sales barriers whilst building long term trusting relationships. It's no coincidence that Jeff has so many enduring relationships, with so many customers, so many years after the initial sales conversation took place. If you have the urge to "strike gold" then start reading, start applying, and start winning the sales outcomes you need and very likely deserve."

"Great motivator and one of the funniest guys I have met, he makes me laugh and has a positive outlook always" Jeff Lewis

Peter Whalley was born in Zimbabwe, nurtured in South Africa, worked in England, France and Germany, and now resides in Australia. In 1996 Peter joined Softline Distribution and as Softline made acquisitions in various global markets; an opportunity arose for Peter to join Australian based Sybiz in 2001 and he has been Managing Director ever since.

Sellativity Makes Sales More Than Just a Numbers Game.

Daryl Blundell
M.D. of Pastel RSA and Sage Pastel International

I started my career in sales, my first job was in the very old, hard world of sales; going "door to door" or "cold calling". Picking up a phone with sweaty, nervous hands and waiting for the next response of "not interested" – being rejected by the umpteenth faceless person of the day.

In the old days, it was all a numbers game; "It's all about activity," our sales managers used to tell us. I can clearly remember always being surprised when people actually gave us their business; it was all very much hit and miss back then!

Then I met this brash "American" named Jeff, who started teaching us how to really sell and what sales should mean. Some of the points I remember clearly and they have always stuck with me:

1. It's about helping people get what they want and in order to do that you need to listen – really listen – to what your clients need.
2. People don't buy on price; they buy on value.
3. As a sales rep, when you provide a client with a quote, you should receive an order in return; if not, you have failed as a sales rep. This really puts a very different spin on the sales process; rather than churning out volumes of quotes.

These are just a few lessons that have stayed with me my sales career.

About Jeff Lewis

I have been working since I was ten years old. I started with a newspaper route, delivering the newspaper six days a week and collecting payment weekly for the afternoon edition of our local newspaper. I did this for five, nearly six years until I began working several part time jobs while attending high school. Needless to say, I had to provide service each day on a time schedule, otherwise I would not get paid, nor increase the number of subscribers on my route.

I learned early to provide good service and be constant and consistent. I did this for nearly six years, through winter, summer, rain, snow, and the ever persistent desire to play with friends rather than deliver the paper. I was able to learn that if I ran and competed against my daily times while delivering the paper, I could get done faster and have more time to play… viola… a discipline and pattern was developed, and I figured it out myself.

I also had a great time playing imaginary football, running with my newspaper sack tucked into my arm and dodging trees, fences, bikes while doing countdowns of the number of steps to the next house, the next yard, etc. I had a great time, got plenty of exercise and earned enough from delivering papers to buy my first car – cash – at fifteen years old, just before my 16th birthday.

Now that I was able to get around, I got myself part-time jobs at Montgomery Ward's department store in the hardware department and then Sears Roebuck became interested because I was fairly knowledgeable and reliable – I showed up every day, a bit unusual for sixteen year old boys in high school. I soon moved to Sears and became the only sixteen year old with authority to approve checks and manage other part-time workers.

This didn't seem to satisfy my work desires so I also took on early morning work at the local Veterinary clinic. I cleaned cages and dog runs and helped prep animals for surgery. All this was done prior to going to school every day. So I worked early morning and later in the afternoon at Sears.

During this time in my life (high school) my mother passed away from cancer and I was somewhat forced into finding more work to support myself as this became a necessity. I managed to squeeze my school schedule together and cut out all the peripheral open periods so I could fit another job into the picture. What ensued was the following daily schedule: 5:30 a.m. – 8:00 a.m. Vet clinic; 8:15 a.m. – 12:45 p.m. School; 1:00 p.m. – 4:00 p.m. Sears; 4:00 p.m. – 12:00 a.m. Gas station (petrol station). Hard to do, maybe, but doable; I guess it was because I did it for more than two years. Was it hard, or more than a teenager should be asked to do? Maybe it was.

However, I certainly learned that you can do more than you think if you dedicate yourself; if you're reliable and enthusiastic. Employers love people who try their best and are enthusiastic about their job. I had no special skills or background for these jobs, and they were diverse, but I won each job interview and each job because I wanted it, and I made sure the employer knew he could rely on me.

I learned to be a good time manager and I learned you could get a lot done in short amounts of time. My work at Sears and then USA Gas had the same 4 p.m. end and start time, so it involved negotiating with both employers to allow a slight bit of flexibility to enable me to leave five minutes early or arrive five minutes late for one or the other on alternate days, thus meaning I had to move quickly to make this work. I also had to get by with not much sleep… maybe sleep was overrated.

Shortly after graduating high school I decided it was time to get on with life. I had already started on a veterinary science animal health technician diploma through my work at the clinic, so it required me to finish the course through the state university and obtain my degree, which I did.

I already knew this was not the career for me and the required time and money to continue on to be a veterinarian seemed long and far away, and expensive for someone providing for themselves at eighteen years old, so I collected my diploma papers and headed for Texas. Work in the steel mills around Houston was booming and the call of the money caught my attention.

The next five years were trying times, hard work, dirty work, ugly work, ugly environment, long hours, hot, sweaty, dangerous jobs that made me realise this was not my calling. Texas Steel was losing its appeal and I transferred back to Ohio, to one of the oldest steel making plants, working in the blast furnace and coke plants. It was horrific, I witnessed men getting their legs burned off from molten steel, I witnessed lots of life-threatening work for the sake of steel... ridiculous to live a life like that. It was sucking the life out of me. Next came the defining moment when my true calling would come find me.

The steel market started to experience serious pressure from the Japanese imports into the USA and the cut-backs and lay-offs began. Soon enough the wave hit me and for the first time in my life I was out of work. What a weird experience; I began searching for what else could be possible for my life. While looking and searching, I worked on horse farms, as a painter and handyman, and I tendered for housing project refurbishments and won the contracts, albeit they were cheap – it kept me working and earning something.

And then THE opportunity came knocking on my door in the form of John from Florida and my calling was clear, once I could convince myself to learn that ten page script – ha! What made this initial journey into sales so much fun was working with my sales manager at that time and the incredible laughs we would have, he was invaluable and a real benefit to me. And then, just to be fortunate to move in and out of human nature on display everyday where you get the chance to walk right into peoples homes and their lives – that cannot be minimised or diminished as a major contributor to my desire to work with people and help lift them up... and through this process, actually lift me up.

During my early direct selling time is when I invested so much time in Zig Ziglar courses, events, materials, books, tapes, and personal attendance at training seminars. What really became apparent through this is that I loved to impart the lessons I was learning to others and soon found that I was a really good teacher. It wasn't long before my success and desire to teach opened the door to becoming a regional sales manager at age twenty-four.

I was assigned to a rural area where farming and small communities were the norm – quite a difference to my city upbringing – and had to quickly recruit, build a team, teach, train and generate sales out of an area which had never been farmed (excuse the farm pun since I was in farm country) before.

What a great time I had with my newly recruited team – the newbie's. Within eighteen months, we became the Number One region in the territory with five of the best salespeople any region had ever seen; all of them became the top five in the state. We had a great time and their success was mine. It was an adventure and each of these guys had families so the entire group became my extended family.

Next I became the sales director for a region on the east coast of the USA, a region which had languished at the very bottom of the USA territories and shown very little promise for nine years in a row. At twenty-seven I was the youngest sales director in a major region, in the history of a company which had roots dating back to the 1860's.

I took this area with the knowledge that it was very difficult to recruit salespeople because it was an expensive place to live. Nevertheless, the challenge was one I wanted, and the result… we went to number three in the USA within thirty months.

We had taken the region to number three in the country from number thirty-two (total number of regions in the USA market). We recruited and grew salespeople from inside the State, we went to S. America and recruited Spanish speaking salespeople; we recruited part-timers, we recruited students and we virtually had an army out there, producing results which were unthinkable little more than two years earlier. Success was achievable with the right attitude and process and it was now time for me to move on to new challenges.

At thirty or thirty-one years old, I entered the oil industry and began a career which took me to S. America, the Caribbean, Europe, Middle East, Egypt, West Africa and finally S. Africa. The challenges were new and exciting – a new industry. Would the lessons learned and the sales process known to me hold up under the spotlight of a new industry?

This was an industry which contained corporate clients and government officials, governing bodies with government requirements and expectations as well as foreign interests and legal issues and new cultures and dynamics. New economies and new budgets, revenue requirements and the great unknowns – could I replicate or set up business in new countries? Well apparently I could, because we did – and very successfully as well. Setting up distribution centers and agencies and business partners and joint ventures and government contracts and legal entities and generating income and producing results while growing profits and a sustainable business followed.

◊   REAL LIFE EXPERIENCE: As a sideline to this… while working on the East Coast USA initially in this new position, I also had the desire to keep my direct selling skills sharp and also wanted to make some additional cash as the east coast is an expensive place to live… so I took a secondary position selling vacation packages (sort of time share, but nicer full vacations over a set period of time). The customers would come to us to see what the package entailed and we would sell them a travel package. This place was a great place to sharpen skills as the customers were diverse and the opportunity called for direct selling decision making salespeople. Salespeople at the company came and went like sunrise and sunset every day. There must have been fifteen salespeople per night on shifts from 5:30 – 9:30 p.m. and the place was jumping with activity. The accepted and permitted sales ratio was 20% success, and failure to achieve this percentage each month would result in the revolving door of salespeople we experienced. Now most people who came to work there THOUGHT they knew how to sell and spent most of their time with customers schmoozing and flirting and spouting off nonsensical attributes of the vacation sites without ever figuring out what the modis-operandi was about the sales process – so they sold a few, missed quite a few and came and went through the doors like most salespeople I have come to know over the years.

For me, this was a great challenge and afforded me the opportunity to re-work my sales process suited to this specific environment. The principles and fundamentals were all the same but it needed adjustments for the particular market. I worked on this within the environment for about a week and then (after much practice at home) went on to achieve a 67% closing percentage for my entire time with them. Needless to say, I was the top salesperson in the company and numbers of salespeople there started to adopt my sales process and produced much better results. The branch ended up increasing their overall sales percentage to close to 35% and became the highlight of the group, all because a little bit of time was taken to understand the process and write it up as a script to a movie… voila – success.

About nine months into the dual role of the two companies I was offered an opportunity to begin overseas travel and overseas business opportunities and obviously I could not continue with the travel sales. Nevertheless, I was grateful for this opportunity and it was one of most memorable and fun experiences – and it was in a part time evening position to boot… so don't ever say you can't earn enough; in sales you can earn as much as you want to! The new opportunities offshore opened doors to me for international business and travel and created a desire to work and live in diverse cultures to experience life as the rest of the world lives. Most people do not get these opportunities or do not take the opportunity when it avails itself, for this I am very thankful and grateful and owe my international business acumen to this time. The people, the food, the cultures, the openness of diverse environments – what an amazing journey.

After several years of this, I caught the wave of the IT industry and moved into the hardware environment with one of the top four hardware providers globally. This was again a new environment and new industry with new regulations and expectations and sales cycles and distribution agents and many factors which could limit success, but did not. Building, growing and developing the sales team, the consultants, the process, and most importantly those global accounts, provided new areas of growth, education and success which was soon visible within a tough environment. My time in hardware was rewarded with the last attributed profitable time period of Company X's operation on the African continent.

During this time I was actively recruited into a growing software environment with a company who had been failing badly and running at huge losses in the international territories they were trying to operate in. I was recruited to turn the ship around and produce success from inside an operation that was losing millions. In our first year of operation under my now tested and true methods we produced a small profit (no small achievement since the company had written off millions of $$$ in losses until this time). The subsequent year we grew enormously and posted quite a sizable profit.

Five years into the program we produced QUITE SUBSTANTIAL PROFITS. We operate in more than fifty countries around the world through a Business Partner Franchise program which incorporates numbers of international partners and they in turn supply and manage a further four-hundred and fifty plus resellers, operators and agents in these fifty countries. Our products and services now represent majority market presence in many of our target countries and profits have achieved growth of more than 30% per annum for the previous three years running!

We now have more than 40,000 customers across the world and I can now see it is time to devote my energies back into selling – actually teaching and training selling – because on a global scale it has never been more apparent. Regardless of our huge success, opportunities are being missed everyday, all attributable to our Business partners being more technical than sales orientated.
So, on to the next journey, writing, teaching sharing my story… just the beginning. I also now have twin little boys, my own little training projects.

Introduction

There are a few affirmations that found me:

- ◊ I am here to teach, I am here to raise others up.
- ◊ My thoughts create my reality.
- ◊ You can have everything you want in life, if you help enough other people get what they want.

These are BIG, broad statements and probably can be applied to each person out there. They could resonate with meaning: like raising your own children, or coaching, or teaching others to be better at what they do. For me, the affirmations are who I am and why I am here. I am more alive when I am coaching, teaching, sharing and mentoring; it's just a fact.

And the times when I am not doing that I find the road tougher to navigate, less attractive and not very fulfilling. This is my calling and I have become quite good at it. I believe this book can help you, entertain you and no matter what you are involved in; at some level everything in this life has a sales aspect. It is important to qualify this one: "You can have everything you want in life, if you just help enough other people get what they want". I borrowed this from Zig Ziglar years ago and it has become a driving force for me. The hope that I can help as many people get what they want, and in the process achieve what I want, is vital to my career in sales and to my life.

"My thoughts create my reality" is a foundation for my beliefs.

The other aspect that I really enjoy is making a decision. There is never a more powerful moment than when you have made a decision. Big or small, making a decision is powerful; it releases endorphins and elevates confidence, feelings of empowerment and being in control of your own destiny. This book is about getting a decision. Deciding to decide, making decisions, and ultimately helping others make a decision.

Getting a decision is the heart of selling, without it there is no sale. Having spent the majority of my work life in connection with selling – sales management, sales training, sales development and now managing my own business – I have been provided with access to thousands of scenarios and situations. These scenarios all add to the value of perspective and possibility. I don't think there are many circumstances I haven't encountered.

You may appreciate the fact that the world of sales, of becoming a sales professional, was not my intention growing up.

My dreams growing up centered on sports, namely baseball and football (American Football), until it became painfully apparent that I was attracted to injuries and simply not good enough to make it a paid profession. Granted, I had to be pounded into submission to realise maybe this was not my professional calling.

And thus sales came calling on me!

Sales professionals have the opportunity to experience something new every time they meet a new prospect. Living and conducting business in more than thirty-five USA states, sixty countries outside the USA and over three-hundred major cities throughout the world is not exaggerated; I have experienced the magic of sales in all these places.

I've seen wonders of the world, I've met kings, presidents, ministers of government, a Pope, business giants, ambassadors, historic figures, and every-day people who are the life and soul of the countries, cities and villages they represent.

Am I overstating what sales can do for you if treated as a true profession? No, I am not. All these places and people are true; names may be changed to protect the innocent – ha, I love how that line is always used on TV shows – but the things I am writing about have happened to me - They're True.

Professional sales is magical; it transforms unclear situations into opportunities, making clear the unclear, making understandable what was previously confusing. Taking unknown facts and arranging them in such a way as to enlighten and educate a customer, helping them feel empowered with information and facts they can comprehend, is a powerful emotion to experience.

The story I have to tell is fun and filled with adventure. It recounts hilarious and unusual situations and real-life activities that highlight lessons being taught and lessons being learned. The keys are available and easy to use, but it does require determination and desire.

From an inauspicious calling I have been extremely fortunate and certainly found my way – even if it found me first. I have experienced the magic of SALES.

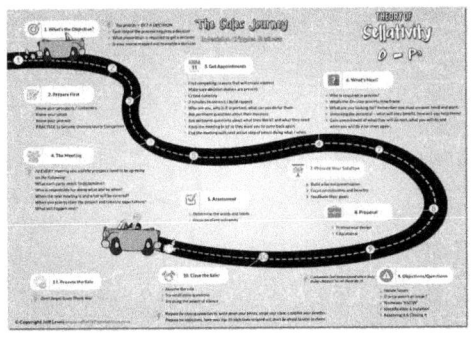

Get your beautiful FREE bonus
"Sales Journey Wall Chart"

Visit
www.sellativitysolutions.com

CHAPTER ONE

The Story Behind the Story

I have enjoyed remarkable experiences stemming from a rather unremarkable upbringing. I was raised in Ohio in the USA, a suburb town reliant on the car industry of the rust belt that was the corridor running from Pittsburg, through Cleveland on to Detroit. My father worked on the assembly line of GM (General Motors) and we lived in a small house on a nondescript street where all the houses and families were relatively the same.

Blue collar middle to lower-middle income families where the father worked, most of the mums were at home and average families were two to four children. Vacations were camping trips, or a short jaunt to something nearby, and otherwise life was the everyday of neighbourhood existence. Growing up I was lucky to hit a time phase that was the baby-boom era and wow did our neighbourhood fulfill that.

Nearly every home had kids so there was a never-ending stream of playmates from every background you could think of; needless to say, adventure presented itself in expected and unexpected ways. Life as a boy on our street was a warp-speed experience.

There was hardly a day that did not have something happen that generated an experience that molded my life. Even as a young boy, before thoughts of selling ever entered my thoughts, I questioned things and wanted to know why. I couldn't accept that just because someone was older that they were an unquestionable authority, it just never sat well with me and led me to many run-ins with teachers and authority figures. Whether it was a concept, a belief or point of view; if someone was pushing their agenda too far I felt uncomfortable and unaccepting – at least until it could be proven.

I loved my young life; it was an adventure and I was the captain of my neighborhood ship. There was not a game we did not play and when we tired of the usual and standard, we created our own. The neighbourhood was our playground and backyards became battlefields, playing fields, and imagination zones that shaped my perception of what the adult world could become. Inflicted and self-inflicted wounds were abundant. We were a physical bunch and a very physical neighbourhood. Even riding bikes down a hill became a competition until it resulted in broken bikes and broken bones.

I would hazard a guess that per capita per kid in our neighbourhood, every child ended up with a broken bone, scar and injury of some sort. The brilliant thing about our group was that hurt feelings or bodies did not last very long and, sooner than you could think of the next game, we were all back together again.

For me, that proved that cooperation and working together is always possible, if you put aside ego and sensitivities and who said what or did what. Get past it and go enjoy life.

As life often dictates, things changed dramatically for me when my mum died of cancer when I turned seventeen. I had been quite a workaholic from a young age, having a paper route from ten years old (and saving enough to buy my first car when I turned sixteen) and then entering a school promoted work scholarship program at sixteen.

I worked my way into juggling three part-time jobs while attending high school. With the ability to set my school schedule I worked for a veterinarian in the early morning from 6am until 8:15am prepping dogs and cats for surgery, cleaning kennels and cleaning surgery areas. In time I worked my way into participating in surgeries.

From there I would race off to school and jam in my subjects before racing off to Sears Roebuck where I worked in the hardware department from 2-4pm and then I would run across the parking lot and worked at USA petrol station from 4-11pm. Needless to say I had a hectic schedule, but it suited me. Through my time at the Vet Clinic I was able to do a correspondence course, apply practical knowledge and go sit the exam at Ohio State University to become a registered Animal Health Technician… which I did.

School for me was a mixed bag, I found some subjects and teachers interesting and others became my playground to perform and question authority, so my time was shared between classrooms and the principal's office. When my mum died my time at home ended pretty suddenly.

My dad found a new partner who came equipped with five of her own kids and my place in the family home ended around six months after my mum died… and thus began my life adventure; finding my own way at a young age.

I had always been a committed and disciplined boy, so finishing school was never in doubt and I found a way to juggle school, work and life on my own until I graduated. That opened creative energies because I had to generate parent signatures for my school reporting. Then the world opened up and offered me a chance to explore. I sought work in Texas that I was accepted for and off I went on my own;

I was eighteen and actually celebrated my nineteenth birthday at work at U.S. Steel working a sixteen hour double shift, shoveling slag out of a rolling pit! When it was over, I went home, collapsed with my legs over the footboard of the bed, fell asleep and was awakened by the phone. As I jumped up to get the phone my legs collapsed completely as if I had been shot. My legs had fallen asleep while hanging over the edge of the bed and I found myself dragging my body over the floor to reach the phone.

It would have made great TV; the shock, the pain, the ridiculous fall and dragging across the floor. That weird moment was a good dose of reality – it was funny, but painful; I was alone and unsatisfied with what I was doing. I was sleep-walking through the early part of my working life and surely I was destined for something better than sixteen hour shifts in a steel slag pile... on my birthday no less!

My time in Texas was shortly to come to an end, I wasn't really a southern boy and definitely not a Texan so back to Ohio and the experience with travel began! On to Oklahoma, back to Ohio, on to New Jersey, Washington DC and then off to Venezuela, Puerto Rico, France, Israel, Egypt, Africa, South Africa and ultimately Australia. Mixed in through all this were hundreds of business trips to hundreds of cities and sixty plus countries.

To say this journey shaped my life would be an understatement. It is, was and has become my life. All these experiences made me who I am. You cannot live, work and experience a country, a culture, a people and not be affected. I am fortunate to have experienced what I have thus far because of one principle – a desire to learn. Each and every stop has offered something new to learn and the fantastic element underscoring all of this was learning to sell and learning what sales are all about. Becoming a sales professional.

When I investigated selling as a career I learned a brutal truth; it was not like being in a factory or assembly line or sitting behind a counter. Either I learned AND applied what I needed to do and started doing it or I was going to be on the welfare line looking for employment and being very hungry with no place to live. For me, I had to succeed; I have never worked in any job that I didn't want to master, so learning how to sell professionally was a "must" for me. I couldn't bear to think otherwise.

So does selling look like this to you?

You are wanting to buy something and you are on the receiving end of someone who is trying too hard; they won't shut up, the pressure is being turned up and you are feeling uneasy, uncomfortable and annoyed. Your frustration grows as you desperately try to find an escape. When will the torture end? You just want the facts so you can make up your own mind. In desperation you request some details in order to get away from the onslaught of information or just walk away saying "I'll think about it" (Sound familiar?).

The so-called salesperson walks away convincing himself that he has done his job, which in his mind consists of crushing you with as many mind-numbing features and descriptions as possible. He has listed every possible attribute, given endless comparisons of competing products, compiled numerous pricing options, related various methods of which you can purchase, finance, put on credit, trade-in, etc. There are limited time guarantees, return policies and, last but not least, discounted options if purchasing inside of a time line.

There is so much being offered that Einstein couldn't even track it all on a chalkboard. It's exhausting and confusing. And all you really wanted was to buy that vacuum cleaner on special. What you end up with is such a complex array of assorted options that you are more confused than when you started and have retreated into your hole to contemplate never vacuuming again. Surely a broom and dust pan has to be easier to manage than making a decision on so many choices.

You don't want to have to hire a consultant to wade through the myriad of options in order to report back on the top-ten most attractive andacceptable choices of vacuum cleaners, do you? So what happened here? What did the information-filled salesperson miss out on in this scenario?

Certainly he supplied the customer with information that the customer asked for, didn't he? He gave them tons of choices, didn't he? He didn't push the customer too hard to buy and he didn't offend them or imply that they couldn't afford it or weren't able to pay. He gave them plenty of brochures and details. The customer even said they had no further questions and just wanted to think about it. Right?

Well, the so-called salesperson thinks he has done a fantastic job and he can now wait right there until the customer returns and hands over their money, because surely, almost certainly, they will be back – right? ………………… WRONG.

Firstly, the fact that the salesperson nearly drove the customer crazy means they are not going back to him again if they can avoid it – that is a statistical certainty 90% of the time. Are you aware that 90% of the time that this type of example plays out, means there is a less than 10% chance the customer will return?

So the salesperson must be repeating this process hundreds of time to generate volume and a multitude of opportunities, thus arriving at a result where a small percentage of customers return – thereby fueling him to continue doing the same thing, because of course someone returned so therefore his method must work. Isn't that horrendously bad habit creation?! You do the wrong thing, someone buys despite what you have done and you condition yourself to continue repeating because it worked once – OUCH!

{My wish for all salespeople is that they never get a "call-back" sale… why? – Because it teaches bad habits. Once you believe customers will think about it and call you back, you are tainted with a bad habit that becomes easy to repeat to your own detriment. DON'T create bad habits, create good habits}.

This type of salesperson is sadly seen as the norm – the teller, not the seller. Customers cannot get specific answers out of him, yet they actually want the product so they buy it. We, as customers, have become the guilty party by perpetuating poor performance and rewarding it with a purchase.

It reminds us of having spoiled children throwing a massive temper tantrum demanding their item of choice and then as wonderful parents, we give in and reward bad behavior with treats. Signaling that the child (or salesperson) can get what they want even if they perform badly. We don't reward good behaviour, we reward bad behaviour. The "salesperson" continues to sell in this manner based on ignorance. No-one teaches, corrects or informs them they are not performing as they should.

I am unaccepting of this bad sales technique, so I now refuse to purchase if the salesperson is not properly equipped to sell. If they are aware enough to ask, I take time to explain why I am not purchasing. The action of purchasing reinforces the salesperson's belief that they are doing a good job and never signals to them that they are not. First lesson, don't reward bad behaviour with success.

My objective is to raise the bar on performance and professionalism in sales people. Shortcuts are for short term success and short term results. In contrast, following the process properly will result in long term results and long term ongoing success.

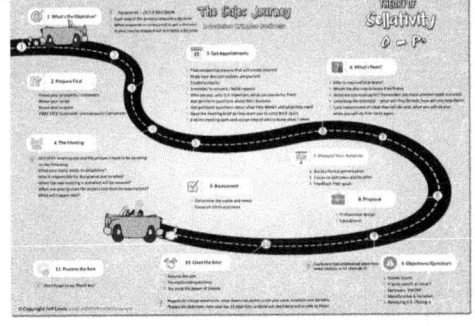

Get your beautiful FREE bonus
"Sales Journey Wall Chart"

Visit
www.sellativitysolutions.com

CHAPTER TWO

The Theory of Sellativity

After years of practice, applying my skills in numerous countries with various cultures and under the worst and best conditions, I realised that a methodology had been built. A precise process developed by hundreds of experiences had emerged. "Sellativity" became reality – just like the theory of relativity. While not easily understood by the masses – nor even easily explainable – once the theory of relativity is broken down and deciphered, it becomes a standard that is applied every day in engineering, scientific research, time and space planning, etc.

The theory of relativity has become the standard application for all practitioners who rely on mathematical principles to establish foundations in their methods. Sellativity had become just that mechanism for me. When I needed to measure against success or the lack of it, resorting back to my theory reflected what I needed to see; it exposed the errors and scars that became visible in the mirror. It shines the light on success and, more importantly, the WHY.

With clarity I can reflect back on my very first true sales call. The first time I accompanied my sales trainer and he pushed me forward at the door of a complete stranger with a simple instruction: "SPEAK". To my sales trainer's credit, he had spent the entire previous day handling every call so that I could watch and gain experience and he had asked me a few times to try it now, to which I kept replying, not yet, do one more, until… "SPEAK" and I had no choice but to say something.

Do you remember summoning up the courage the first time you had to call that special girl or boy to ask them out on a date?

(With texting today and the social media tools available to everyone, perhaps girls or boys don't need this skill anymore, but I remember when it was quite a courageous act) Have you ever been called upon to speak at school, in front of family or in public? These type of events all conjure up the same memories: anticipation, nervousness, apprehension, fear and exhilaration. The adrenaline fires and all kinds of things start happening; an array of good, bad and ugly – ha!

Events where you may be called upon to perform become defining moments in your life. These situations can be very motivating and exciting, or terrifying and paralysing.

You may experience complete meltdown, people may think you are a babbling fool, or it might well be an overwhelming success if you are prepared. Here is a helpful insight for you: The "Theory of Sellativity" is a proven formula - not just theory or numerous alternatives – it is a method that is tested and proven. It is a method that can be trusted and relied upon. Imagine having the formula that can be applied to these situations in order to avoid the dreaded… failure.

The "Theory of Sellativity" will help you build the ability to manage whatever situation arises in your personal or professional life. Maybe you just want to improve your people skills. Maybe you want to improve your ability to take charge of your life, or take charge of your career. Maybe you want more self-confidence and the ability to control your emotions and behavior.

Or just maybe, you want to become that top sales professional – the one who succeeds because he is genuine and professional! The one who continues to grow and work on his profession, the one who makes everyone he sells to or works with feel special and important.

You do know of course, that sales professionals – true sales professionals – are some of the most highly paid professionals in the world and rank in the top earners globally.

Because sales professionals rely on their abilities and skills, there is no limit or ceiling on what they can earn and achieve. If they are able to sell more, they are able to earn more, and that is about the best achievable earning potential any person could ask for, isn't it?

Selling professionally is magical – like alchemy – creating something of value from what was once something without value.

Some people look at sales and it seems confusing or too vast, too many theories like too many stars in the night sky. How and who can see the constellations, what does it take to locate these stars?

How does one navigate the Milky Way of sales?

The theory of 'Sellativity' is a like a GPS guide, allowing you to find a star in the midst of thousands. In a world where there are hundreds of sales methods, processes and procedures, it becomes almost impossible to look into that night sky and find what you are looking for.

Thus, my theory of 'Sellativity' emerged from the dense Milky Way of universal sales processes to become a clear and specific theory. Years of developing sales processes enabled me to establish a clear vision. This vision included a theory to be implemented and utilized - easy to be seen, easy to follow, easy to track and yes, easy to use.

So what is the formula (relativity is $E=MC^2$)

THE THEORY OF 'SELLATIVITY' is: $O = P^3$

The formula broken down:

Objective = PREPARATION x PROCESS x PRACTICE

O = the Objective:
Get a Decision… this is your quest, your 'holy grail' of sales. It is a 100% all-consuming quest to "get a decision". If nothing else makes an impact in this book, understand that the simple task of asking for a decision – asking for the order – will increase sales more than 10%. The simple act of asking for the decision or the order will increase sales results, even if your process was less than impressive.

P= the Preparation:
Preparing a script and strategy. Think through the possible situations, the flow of the conversation, the questions and answers, the obstacles, the roadblocks, the objections… the plan.

P= the Process:
Outlining the 'how to' steps. Taking your preparation time along with the strategy behind it and outlining the steps it will take to achieve the objective.

P= the Practice:
Putting your preparation to practice. The old adage, practice makes perfect is especially true in sales. Practice and practice and practice again. Practice out loud so you can hear your inflection, practice in your head so you can visualize the process. Practice in front of a mirror so you can see your expressions, practice in front of a friend, a colleague, a sales professional… but practice.

LIFE LESSON 1:

My sales career began with a knock on my door. Standing before me was a good sized guy with long mutton chop sideburns, mustache and tinted sunglasses. I glanced at his car and all the windows were tinted too.

I assumed from his license plates that he was from Florida. "Quite a long way from home, aren't you?" I said. He didn't quite catch where I got that from and simply said "are you Jeff Lewis?" Obviously I was and he gave his name in return and then said: "I'm here to help you get started selling. You were referred to me through a friend of yours – can I come in and talk to you?" and he proceeded to step through the door.

There it was – simple, direct and to the point… not may I, not are you interested, not even are you aware that I was coming? Just straight to the point. And with that I let him in.

In the next thirty minutes I was informed about the sales program that 'John' would initiate and how he worked. John informed me that he was recently recruited from Florida to my area with the express purpose of building a sales team and I was first on his list.

Now whether that is true or not I do not know to this day, but saying I was first on his list made an impression and it certainly made me feel important.

John said that our "mutual friend" thought I was well suited to sales and that I would like to give it a try.

At the time, I was seriously considering a career change and I did have some interest in sales, but when John said to me it was strictly commission, no salary and no medical plan or benefits unless I sold a certain amount each month, I felt my heart sink and nausea quickly became evident. The thought of strictly commission and no salary for someone who had been working since they were ten years old seemed harsh, unfair and very risky.

With this I was ready to toss this idea in the bin, when John said something that struck me. He told me I would never find more opportunities, freedom to go wherever I wanted to go and the complete feeling of being in control of my life than when I relied on my abilities and got paid what I truly deserved based on my own effort, without being reliant on an employer to pay me what he thought I was worth.

Then came the determining challenge. I will draw your attention to our theory: the 'O' for Objective and the first 'P' for preparation...

John told me he would give all the help I wanted and he would work with me until I got it right once I did the following:

1. **'O'** – make a decision that I wanted to do this. A commitment to myself that I would dedicate the time and effort to learn how to sell. The "Decision" was the all-important factor.

2. **'P'** – once I made that decision, I had to memorize a ten page typed manuscript which John called his canvas, or his script. He said that until I proved to myself through memorizing the script that I was serious about this career change, that he wouldn't take me serious either and wouldn't come back to help me. So the decision was mine.

The next four weeks were troubling times, wrestling with the decision. Pulling the script out, reading it, trying to memorize it, putting it away, asking myself who I was kidding, asking nobody in particular who would be able to memorize this entire script word for word. I mean really, who was John kidding, certainly he did not really mean word for word, did he? I phoned and told John I had the gist of it and had adapted it to my personality, he said fine, I could start anytime I wanted without him.

Until I learned it exactly as he had prepared it he wasn't coming to help get me started. (He was closing wasn't he? And he wasn't giving in, he held firm to his promise). Frustration and anger turned to resolve when I realised he was serious about this and I started dedicating time to learn the script completely.

During this time I began to notice little things that were being said in the script that seemed to make a point, and this is when I was able to claim the 'O' in the objective – I made a decision.

I would do this, and do it 100%. Up to this point, during this four-week struggle, I found I could not concentrate, I could not choose any direction for my life and I couldn't move forward because I was stuck in "in-decision". That terrible place where depression sets in, self-doubt arises, crisis appears and nothing seems to go right in your life.

This is what in-decision does; it robs you of the ability to focus, to move forward, to be confident, clear and self-assured. Until you make decisions in your life you are like a boat drifting in the sea. When decisions are made, the picture suddenly clears, things come into focus, and clarity arrives along with self-confidence and assurance. Once I made this decision, I was free to concentrate on becoming a salesperson and put away all the doubts.

It still took a further two weeks, but when that next call went to John, I said I was ready; I had learned the script and wanted to get started. He said he would be there Monday morning to test me, and if I was indeed ready we would begin that week. I was and we did, and the next chapter will reveal one of the classic stories in the book of overcoming fear and procrastination, but that is for the next chapter… for now, lets see how the lesson set the tone of the first components of the 'Theory of Sellativity'.

We are starting with the 'O' and the first 'P'. The objective is to get a decision and the first 'P' is preparation. Without John calling for a decision and directing me to the fact that until I made a decision, he could not and would not help me, I would have wandered around somewhat aimlessly for who knows how much longer in my life. I, along with many others in this world got used to just living while going through the motions. Not really motivated, energised, enthusiastic, nor excited about life. Just 'getting by' as they say.

This is often due to the fact that decisions are pending, choices are in a holding pattern in your head and procrastination and delay set in. You'd rather do the easy thing and just go about your daily existence instead of making a choice; a determined decision to do something different or unique, or at least more suited to YOU.

One other thing was learned from this, first impressions can be overcome – but why fight through this roadblock and obstacle if you don't need to. John's initial appearance could have put me off, but his personality and true self shone through. I got to know him as a friend, a mentor, a manager, a counselor, and a genuinely great guy over the years we worked together – but it could have gone very wrong from the outset because John chose to present himself in a very specific appearance. Over time, even John realised that a more professional look actually improved his results.

The main focus of this chapter is the fact of the preparation – which we will cover as we continue – and the fact is, from the minute John introduced the program to me, he had prepared the process it would take to get me ready. He had done the work to prepare a script that he knew would establish the foundation I required to begin my career. Without this, I am certain beyond any doubt that I would have floundered and evolved with bad habits, bad preparation and mediocre results.

Even if I were to become really confident about this profession, without preparation I would have been like the thousands of others who just pick up the product and start selling. For me, the six weeks required to get my decision in place and then commit myself to learning the script were more important than the next few years of selling.

I learned that once I knew every aspect of what was going to take place, I never needed to feel lost or at a loss for words. I had them all ready and waiting and I was PREPARED for any eventuality that would come my way… and believe me, they did, you'll see.

Later on I will relate some of the stories that took place and you will see that preparation was the saving grace – sometimes the comedic saving grace – but nevertheless, the preparation done today will save you tomorrow. Learn that lesson and it will serve you well.

So, let's get on with it. What is 'Sellativity' all about?

'Sellativity' starts and ends with the understanding that sales is a profession.

Just like medicine, accountancy, teaching, engineering and professional sports. Think about each of these professions and what it requires to attain the title of professional of any of these fields. As each profession has it methods, procedures and processes – so does the sales profession. The question isn't whether you believe this, the question is what you will do with this fact now that it is being presented to you. That sales is often not viewed as a profession in the same level reference of the aforementioned sectors is a statement of society.

Most businesses today approach sales and salespeople as a necessary evil. They attempt to pay low salaries, incentivise and commission load the salesperson and cross their fingers that they have hired the right people to do the job and achieve the sales they require in the business.

Companies then assert the position that salespeople close approximately 20% of their attempts and set this as the benchmark for commission and retention of the salesperson's position in the company. Nice job security and satisfaction, eh? Just how motivating is the fact that 20% sales closure equals satisfied results – hmmm, makes you wonder already doesn't it?
Note: are you aware this is the standard acceptable closure rate for salespeople just about everywhere in the world? Who set this and accepted this to be so, I want to know…

And how much training and teaching does the new salesperson receive? A bit of product training, a bit of internal guidance with "experienced" salespeople in the position, or perhaps a bit of coaching or training from the sales manager? Generally very sketchy and less than comprehensive assistance is provided before the salesperson is set loose to "go sell". This continues to be the accepted practice of business and salespeople in today's business world.

Aha – that was all before this guide to 'Sellativity', which is designed to alter the perception of both business and salespeople. All that is required is structure, knowledge with understanding, procedures, process and practice along with some time devoted to learning this profession. You wouldn't go to university for a medical degree if it wasn't going to help you in your medical career would you? And you wouldn't enter the medical practice profession if you didn't know what you were doing would you? (Well, maybe you might, but how long would you last if you didn't know what you were doing? do you think your patients or customers would keep coming back?)

'Sellativity' is an art-form, a design, a practice, a profession – just like a surgical procedure or an accountancy practice. It is a method which once learned is the same as any other profession, skills are developed, process is learned, procedures are followed, knowledge is applied and results are forthcoming – results which are successful and expected, just like a surgical procedure.

Just as Einstein developed the theory of relativity based on years of research and trials and testing, so I have developed the theory of 'Sellativity' based on the same principles. More than twenty-five years of research and trials has gone into my 'Sellativity' methods in more than fifty countries through more than seven major industries that I have worked within (books, encyclopedia's, oil, travel, freight, logistics, computer hardware, computer software and consulting). Developing methods across such a broad spectrum of industry types teaches you how to mold and define techniques based on sales principles applied to the different industries.

Direct sales – such as selling books, encyclopedias, travel packages – demand trust-making conversational skills which rely on immediate decision making. Short sales cycles, such as small business solutions, demand investigative- and needs-analysis skills reliant on relationship skills which generate confidence in your technical and solution skills along with the ability to gain decisions from a few select decision-makers over a short-term period of meetings and follow-ups. Long sales cycles, such as computer systems and hardware deployment, require relationship management, management of technical resources, multiple decision makers, multiple requirements by multiple individuals or departments and the ability to orchestrate and manage multiple decision-makers, resulting in a conclusive decisions.

Putting these methods to the test in all the regions, countries, cities and cultures where I have lived and worked has given me plenty of background with negotiation and selling skills across various customs. Testing methods in diverse cultures develops understanding and insight into the sales process like testing in the fire. When you are dealing with varying perspectives and accepted practices and customs it is as if you are attending university and studying from a learned professor.

Thus, 'Sellativity' is method or theory, if you will, of following the process through interaction with the customer in a conversational manner. This customer can be represented as a client, a prospective interest, an acquaintance, a business partner or student. What this really says to us is that we need to learn our craft, our profession, just like any other.

Study, knowledge, application of that knowledge, process, procedure, and practice are the key elements. Once understood that the sales profession is a profession of substance and one which can accelerate your growth experience locally or internationally the student becomes an avid disciple of the methods which lead to success.

The theory simply validates that the Objective = Preparation times Process times Practice ($O=p^3$).

This means that in order to ensure you always reach your objective, you must properly prepare (design a script/presentation/procedure), based on solid principles and past performance examples, you must then practice and keep practicing consistently AND you must follow the process time after time.

Rely on your process once you have refined it and honed it to perfection. The conversational interaction between you and the customer is the glue that connects you and allows you to assess and assist the customer to reach the objective.

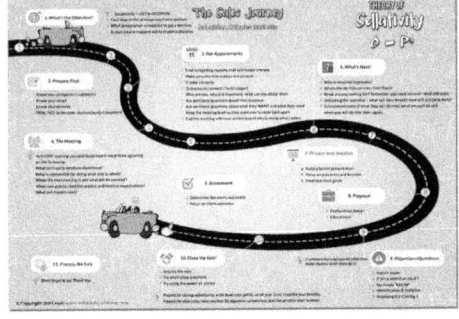

Get your beautiful FREE bonus
"Sales Journey Wall Chart"

Visit
www.sellativitysolutions.com

CHAPTER THREE

Preparation

So let's prepare you to prepare. Here's where you build the foundation for your process.

Like building a house, the foundation is critical to the long term success and the more planning you do here, the more successful you will be. Time taken in the plans, the details and the effect will determine the outcome. Preparing your sales plan becomes fun - like fitting the right pieces into the puzzle on the road to a finished product.

You know now that you have an objective – get a decision – you know that to get a decision you need to have a good sales process to lead the customer to a good decision. In order to create a good process you need to be prepared:

Preparation is all about analyzing and assessing all aspects of the sales process and then establishing the absolute best process possible to help you achieve your objective. Are you already thinking of what you are going to say? It's exciting isn't it? Like writing your own movie and you are starring in it, every day!

One thing I learned very early, sales as a profession can be learned just like any other profession you attend school for. Accountants, rocket scientists, teachers, doctors, dentists, surgeons, engineers, nurses, economists, politicians and athletes, all share two common traits – training followed by practice.
Years of school to impart knowledge followed by internships and apprenticeships all lead to what is required in order to be successful – training and practice.

I began every day with rehearsing the sales process, orchestrating the new additions and working on methods to overcome objections. This involved projecting images of situations and then managing those situations through preparation – preparing answers and explanations for every possible objection or alternative situation that might arise. You know how sometimes movies have alternative endings? The writer may have two or three ways that the movie might end and they film them all to see which has the best effect or makes the most sense.

The preparation of all the alternative endings is scripted out with various situations creating the subsequent desired result. For you, the reading and writing of these important questions form the backbone of your sales process. A few assorted practice tips to warm up before venturing out:

- "what will you say?" AND "how will they respond?""
- "what could they say?" AND "how will you respond?"

I am going to outline a few examples of various scenarios, whether it is direct sales or consulting related… J (that will be me, Jeff) & C (that will be customer).

Initial contact (direct book sales - but it can be applied to most any type of direct selling now days too):

J – Hi, my name is Jeff and I am here on behalf of XXXX company, we are busy in your area talking with families interested in finding better ways to help educate and prepare their kids while growing up. I'm sure that as parents you are always looking for creative and new ways to help your children, may I come in and talk with you for a few minutes?

[a couple things to note – I stress the fact that using the word 'better' in the above example is an option… not that any parents are not doing a good job already, but the fact that there might be a 'better' option, or method. Also, the fact that I take an assumptive active position by stating that I am sure they are such a parent, and based on that assumption, they would be interested. For them to say no creates a conflict in their mind due to the fact that their reasoning will say to them that if they say no, they are possibly saying they are not interested in their child, nor interested in investigating possible "better" options. And based on my assumptive active approach, I simply break eye contact, reach for the door and take a step forward. The customer generally agrees and allows entry based on this series of events].

When they do not agree, they may say….

C – Hold on a second, what is it you are doing or selling?
J – Pardon me, I may not have been very clear, my name is Jeff Lewis, and I am with XXXX, we have an established service for parents that has been around for more than XX years and we have found that parents such as yourself enjoy the opportunity of seeing what we have to share with them regarding their children's education, morals and decision making ability. Today's environment certainly does put a lot of pressure on our kids to perform or conform to pressures of other kids, peers, school and even parents. That is why we have developed such a program designed for parents who care. I would appreciate just a few minutes of your time to ask you a few questions and show you some of our findings; would you have just a few minutes for me to visit with you?

[And with this, I once again break eye contact and move forward toward the door. Once again the assumptive active position enforces that you believe they agree with you and want to see what you have to say].

Another possibility of the customer may go like this:

C - "I'm not interested".

J – Well, I can't blame you; I haven't said much that is very interesting thus far, have I? (With a laugh and a smile!)……may I ask you whether you have children? (This is designed to slow them down and engage them in conversation)
C – Yes I do; two kids.
J – Fantastic, may I ask how old?
C – Two and four.
J – Wow, that is a handful of high speed, non-stop activity, isn't it? I'm sure they keep you busy and running all the time, don"t they?
C – Yes they do, and I hardly have time for anything else….
J – That is exactly why we designed our service, for mum's just like you. I know you are busy, but I am sure just a few minutes could really open your eyes to some really useful information.

Being as busy as you are, you may not always have time to go investigate what is available today to help, and we are able to bring some of that information directly to you without you having to leave the house and it only takes a few minutes… I'm sure that would be helpful to you, may I come in and I promise to be quick… [Once more, take the assumptive active position and break eye contact and move toward the door].

With this, I am sure you get the idea. There are many and numerous directions the conversation can take you. The key is to be prepared with numerous rehearsed scripts based on possibilities of what the customer may say. If you sit down and mentally picture the process, you will realise that once you put a solid professional entry script in place, one that encapsulates several possible customer responses, it becomes easier to polish your script to remove obstacles and possible interruptions from the onset.

You will notice in my opening script that many objections or roadblocks had already been considered and the script afforded me a very solid and high percentage opportunity of gaining entry. And if it didn't, the possible objections or rebuffs from the customer could be anticipated and prepared for through role play in the mental preparation. Think about it... based on a good entry approach, how many possible responses could the customer provide? The responses encompass either a 'yes' or a 'no'. If it is yes, then you are in and you proceed to the next phase. If it is no, what might the 'no' responses sound like? As I have pointed out above, the roadblocks or objections can be systematically played out, like in a movie. There are the general standard objections that revolve around the following:

- ◊ not interested
- ◊ no time (not now)
- ◊ what is it about
- ◊ are you trying to sell me something
- ◊ we are well equipped to handle our children

With each of these, you are able to prepare a response and a re-approach to once again gain the appointment, or opportunity to move to the next step. It only takes a little imagination and foresight to envisage what possible responses might be forthcoming, and then you can prepare for it. As an exercise in your growth experience with sales as a profession, take a few minutes to write down what responses you would develop based on these objections. Make sure you keep it positive, professional and most of all, driven toward the objective of getting that decision… and hopefully a "yes" decision to allow you to continue.

Take some time to review each of your answers and repeat the objection and your response out loud while assuming the role of the customer. With this in mind, would you let 'you' in the door? If not, work on the wording, the rhythm, the impact and ensure you keep that confident, assumptive position in mind. Remember, the goal is not to sell them on the doorstep, the goal is only to gain entry based on this scenario.

Here is another telesales option involving software and the opportunity to obtain an appointment.

Once again, a number of responses or objections could be forthcoming, if your initial script is not top shelf. You be the judge, what would you add, subtract? What would you say if you were the customer… and what would you say if you were responding to the customer's objection?

Example, Initial contact software sales:

Mr. X: One of the best things about technology and software is the fact that it gives us as consumers and customers the ability to "choose" the "best" solution for our business today. Years ago, choices were limited, but today efficiency and cost options provide us with the best opportunity to ensure we are getting the "best" out of our solutions.

I am sure you feel you are making good decisions everyday in regards to your business. What if it were possible that there might be even "better" solutions available to you that you are not aware of ?………. Surely you would at least want to take a look, yes?

In a nutshell, that is all we are offering – the chance to take a look at a solution that MAY help you manage your business even "better" than what you are doing presently, and I am sure you would appreciate the chance to at least take a look, yes?

(Wait for them to agree with you) they will ask questions now… be prepared to provide very short answers, and keep driving them back to a demo, an opportunity to meet and show them, the opportunity to send them the demo, etc.

DO NOT try to sell the product over the phone, and do not give lengthy features descriptions over the phone!!! Get them to your objective, which should be:

A demo meeting / an appointment of some type.

You can always email feature lists, comparatives, brochures, etc. but be very careful here – the old saying is – if the brochure can do my job, then why do they need me?! The brochure, feature lists are only an aid to help you cement the interest, not to sell for you! YOU must sell and the only way to do this is to see the customer!

At this point, ask how you can help…… (Now you are helping him, not selling him)… and offer no more than three choices:

1. May we set a time for me to meet you and quickly present the solution we offer, we need no more than one hour….What times would be most suitable? (offer two times/ dates)
2. May we send our consultant to answer your questions and assess how we might be of service to you in your quest to continually improve your business? We find that like with any new product, a little insight and assistance goes a long way to really understanding what the solution can do for you…
3. May we set a time to 'bring' you a demo CD and drop off a bit more information? (obviously this is a subtle way to get an appointment to see them without being too direct).

Keep it short, create interest and curiosity, and GET an APPOINTMENT – that should be your objective. What you are doing in this script is commending them on being a good decision maker, a wise businessman who chooses well and makes good decisions on his software. You are telling him he is good at what he is doing, and through this process of building his ego, you are subtly inferring that if he is so wise then he will not want to dismiss an opportunity to see IF he could have something better than what he has now!

You are saying he has "good" and maybe he could have "better" or "best" – that appeals to his ego and will drive him to be curious. In a mild way you are challenging him to prove he is a good businessman.

You can always rely on the fact that you are using "good, better, best" as options. This appeals to everyone if used correctly. You say he has good, maybe even better than good, BUT what if he could have "best"?! And of course if it is cost effective, then what a bonus!

You may ask why this would be important; well consider an athlete, who warms up before a performance or game. They stretch, jog around; loosen up in preparation for the upcoming game or event. Prior to that day's game or event, training takes place for months, days and hours on end to perfect their activity. Films of their performance are studied, their methods are refined, and they are coached and trained while studying game plans. They study, they research, and they investigate their opponents – all this in preparation for the forthcoming game which is the reason for their training.

And so I figured that if an athlete needs to prepare and train, and then loosen up prior to going out there, then I needed to do the same – and I did.

Before you begin the process of fully understanding what the foundation is to professional selling, let's establish what the ground rules are for your participation in this journey.You will need to prepare your sales process, your script and your presentation. Here are a few points to consider as you map out your strategy:

When I was to begin selling I was given that script to memorise. Ten type-written pages, word for word memorisation. I was told I would not be allowed to go sell until I learned it completely and I would be tested by my sales manager weekly until I got it right. Now think about this concept for a minute – in acting a full and complete script is given to the actors which they must also learn word for word. Why is that? It is because the writer has a flow, a direction that he is taking the viewer through during the course of the play or movie.

He is taking the viewer (the customer) on a journey and the writer wants to ensure the plot has a theme and a flow and direction and it leads the viewer (the customer) to an ending… a conclusion… an objective.

The writer inserts everything into this script: how he wants the scene set, where the actor enters from, the mood, the setting, the lighting, and even the manner in which he wants the actor to enter; is he angry, happy, concerned, anxious, uptight, etc. The writer continues with how the words are spoken, in what context, in what manner; heated, softly, with pain, with sorrow, etc. It further details the actions taking place; is the actor sitting, standing, kneeling, lying down, is the actor speaking with a pained look on his face, is he smiling, serious, smirking, uneasy.

Every single detail of the scene is written and described. Detailed to the maximum extent in order to set the scene and prepare the actor for what needs to happen during his role on the stage or set. And the writer or director manages the process meticulously to ensure he captures the ultimate enactment of the scene in order to portray to the viewer (the customer) the intent of the scene, the direction of the scene and the mood of the scene.

The director may insist on numerous practice sessions or 'takes' and may isnsist on numerous shots or angles taken to film in order to capture the best representation of the scene. Actors, writers and directors work in unison to ensure they have captured the spirit of the story through all various scenes through the project and they arrive with a finished project. They arrive at the end – the objective – because they followed the script and worked on it throughout to ensure they captured the best adaptation of every scene.

This manner of working has been tried and tested and ensures success in this industry. 'Sellativity' is successful following the same process.

If the movie and theater business is geared around scripts and defined process for each and every scene, why not sales?

Back to my story – I was required to learn this script word for word because it was to form the foundation for all I was about to encounter. It was the base from which I would work and became the rock that I could cling to when I stumbled or fell. It would provide the base for me to refer to and find my way again; to get me back on course and allow me to find my place and continue.

At first, trying to learn this script was frustrating and I would often exclaim that it was ridiculous and who needed this – just let me go sell. In hindsight, it was the best thing I ever did to learn that script word for word. When I had that script memorised, I knew why I was saying certain things at certain times – it all made sense. One statement or question led to another which led to another which led the customer to the objective. And it was like a conversation, a duet, an interaction between me and the customer that incorporated us both and made us work together.

How many times do you see a presentation or sales pitch and the person is just talking 'at' you? They are so intent on just making sure they spew out all their wonderful points that they do not involve you at all. What is very sad is that they remove their observation skills and do not seek to evaluate and asses their performance, otherwise they would recognize what they are doing and change it!

Think again of acting in a play or a movie – it gets reviewed and assessed. From this the actor makes changes, grows, learns and adapts – as do the writers and directors – until they perfect their skills and win awards for their achievements. What about you, Joe S. Salesperson?

Back to my story again to finish this extremely important point: once the foundation was in place with a process from start to finish, I could then work on aspects of the process which needed refinement and alteration. Through the script I was able to recognise places where I could add in questions or commitment requests.

Through the script I was able to recognise that more often than not I would hear a particular objection or non-commitment and this allowed me to assess the process and the script and make changes. I would sit every morning and review my previous day's activities – my notes from each presentation… what did I say, what did they say, how did they respond, what objections, what did I say to these objections, how did we conclude, what close did I use, how did they react, etc. (refer to earlier in the chapter examples).

Because I knew my script so well, it was easy to recognise what part the customer had to play when they interjected and what they had to say.

It became easy to replay these events and then start to map out what I needed to do to make changes.

And I would write it down – just like a script in a play. Word for word, I would write what I wanted to say and what reaction or reply I could expect from the customer, and depending on what answer they might give, I would script my next line.

I would work on the rhythm and how it was phrased, how I would say it, with what emphasis and intonation. I would practice the script to see how it sounded – was it conversational, was it comfortable, was it pleasant, and was it effective?! I would write and practice and write and practice until I would get it just right. Then it would become part of my new script and I would track the results.

Listen to your presentation, Listen to your script, Listen to yourself! Get a recorder and practice your script – listen to it and critique yourself. What sounds believable, what doesn't? What sounds convincing, what doesn't.

What sounds comfortable and conversational and what doesn't. Record your entire script as if you are actively selling – use your voice inflections, use your emotions, your change of pace, your questions, your requests, your benefits, your closing sequence – record it all. And then listen to it, make notes, listen again... what is missing, what needs refinement, what changes need made? Could you say it better, could you ask the question better, and can you assist the customer in arriving at a decision better? Listen, listen listen.

Nothing will make you professional more than practice and listening to what you are saying.

An example is the "I'll think about it" objection from customers. I worked and worked on this one to find a place in my opening script where the process would be smooth, but the impact would be effective. I cover the actual process of this in the upcoming chapter, but suffice it to say that writing, preparing and practicing your process is essential to great success.

It becomes the foundation of your confidence and allows you to concentrate on the customer and the customer's responses because you are prepared and know by heart what you are doing. I worked on this one until I knew every single word had impact, every pause and change of intonation had purpose, every aspect of the message had to be exactly perfect.

Like the stick shift car – once you have mastered it, it becomes an unconsciously competent process you follow every single time you drive. The sale process is the same – get into the process of building and creating your process – it will be one of the greatest things you ever do for you. So let's go to the next chapter to look at this thing called The Process.

Theory of Sellativity *Preparation*

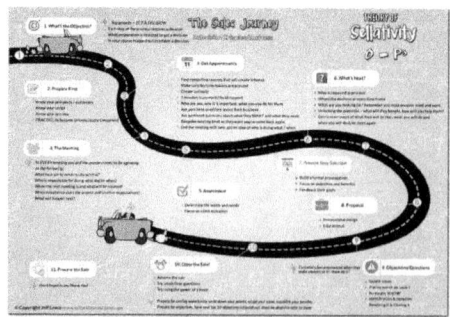

Get your beautiful FREE bonus
"Sales Journey Wall Chart"

Visit
www.sellativitysolutions.com

CHAPTER FOUR

Process

Where to begin, what is the key in the process? What is the process?

Well, here is a straightforward definition of PROCESS:

Process (as Noun)

1. Series of actions – a series of actions directed toward a particular aim.
2. Series of natural occurrences – a series of natural occurrences that produce change or development.

Process (as Verb)

1. Prepare something using a process – transitive verb to treat or prepare something in a series of steps or actions, for example, using chemicals or industrial machinery.
2. Use procedures to do something – transitive verb to deal with somebody or something according to an established procedure.

Our sales process is most certainly encompassed within the noun definition…..a series of actions directed toward a particular aim. Excellent, I couldn't have said it better myself. It is also encompassed within the verb definition…..a series of steps or actions.

Now let's look at the definition of our first P = Preparation.

PREPARATION:

(as Noun)

1. Preparing someone or something – the work or planning involved in making something or somebody ready or in putting something together in advance
2. Readiness – a state of readiness… Twenty place settings lay carefully arranged in preparation for the guests
3. Preparatory measure – something done in advance in order to be ready for a future event.

Our sales preparation is most certainly understood within the definitions given, especially as it relates to #3 – something done in advance in order to be ready for a future event. Let's have a look at some of the aspects of both Process and Preparation in selling and see where they fit:

1. Assess your sales type (preparation)
2. Begin your script based on the sales type (process & prep)
3. Learn your product and your script (prep)
4. Practice your script – listen to your presentation (prep)
5. Prepare your materials and documents (prep)
6. Initiate your sales process – tele appointments, cold calling, etc. (process)
7. Make that first sales call / meeting (process)
    a. first impression
    b. first three minutes
    c. introduction of yourself and your business
8. Presentation (process)
9. Q&A (process)
10. Close (process)
11. Objections (if any) (process).

With this in mind, here is an example of a process to establish the necessary preparation required…

PROCESS PREPARATION:

Establish what type of sale you will pursue:

- ◊ A direct, one-call sales opportunity
- ◊ A consulting type multi-call sales opportunity
- ◊ A limited number of meetings-type sales call opportunity.

Why am I asking you to do this? If you are not clear on what type of sales process you are entering into, how can you prepare the right script? The major difference, of course, with a direct one-call sales opportunity is that you must incorporate all the information along with a call to action and call for a decision.

Now this can be tricky if you just plow ahead with your presentation and at the end then spring the call for a decision on them without warning. Perhaps they think you are just showing them something and you will come back again when it is time to make the sale. Therefore, it becomes very evident that you better prepare them and lay the foundation for asking for a decision. The issue of customers wanting to "think about it" must be addressed in both types of scripts and can be adjusted to cover for both.

I learned years ago that the most frequent objection or stall tactic or reason for not making a decision is the famous – " I want to think about it" objection.

Once delivered by the customer, the sales person is then fighting an uphill battle because this objection is so broad and so vague. What is it that the customer wants to think about – cost, price, benefits, and features, will it work, do I want it, and do I need it? These are just a few, and you can of course start the process of answering the objection and asking the right questions and begin the process of fighting your way back to a decision (we will cover this and more objections in the next chapter).

However, during my sales apprenticeship while working on my own, during the course of a particularly hard stretch of no sales, early in my start-up days, I discovered this priceless insight… why not make that annoying objection go away so I don't hear it anymore? Like a blast of cool air on a sweltering summer day, this idea jumped out at me during a short break one day.

The setting was such that I was working a particular sub-division in a small town and I had repeatedly heard a specific objection in a succession of homes. How was I able to recognise this was the reason I was not getting sales?

Through reading and perfecting my script and through reading Zig's books on handling objections I came across the most revealing fact. If you incorporate particular objections into your script at the outset and raise them prior to the customer raising them, you can control it (the objection) and get it out of the way, through customer acceptance and approval.

The penny dropped! I quickly hauled out my notepad and dug into my recap of sales calls during the last three weeks. What was the defining pattern… what did I say, and then what did they say… what objection was most obvious…

and there it was: "I want to think about it". In a variety of ways, the same objection was coming through time and time again. Whether it was one parent wanting to discuss with another, or the need to check the funds, or wanting to sleep on it, or wanting to go through the material to decide which the right choice was. Whatever variation it was, it was the same thing over and over.

The customer would love my product and service, but then would haul out the "I want to think about it" objection and while with some of them I was able to work through and still get a positive conclusion, the fact was that this objection was causing major concern and taking a lot of time to overcome and it was taxing on me and the customers, with more non-successful outcomes than successful outcomes.

I was determined to figure out what was causing this, and so I poured over my script trying to uncover what trigger was calling for this response. What was I doing to bring about this response? What did I say and what did they say… and what was in my script that was inviting this response?

And then I saw it, almost everything in my script and presentation was geared to sharing information, which was not a bad thing, but in this case it was also the death knell because I was so busy making sure I 'shared' the information that the customer was relaxed into just listening and there was no call for the customer to participate or for the customer to know that they had a role to play, which was to make a decision at the end.

I sat there and began looking for the right place to interject my "objection buster". [This should once again confirm the importance of a script.

Without it, I would be hunting in the dark for the place to say what I needed to say, and each sales call could call for a placement of this very important request, so without a script, the solution would not have been possible]. The thought I had was that if the customer could be shown the value of making a decision in the present tense without even asking for a delay, then we could get on with satisfying everyone.

The way to do that was to ask them to help me with the problem.

A few points should be realised here. The fact that a script is invaluable and the fact that keeping a record of your sales visits is equally important. A running assessment of each opportunity can help you see what is going right and what is going wrong. The need to sit down and assess when things are not clicking is important, and the need to fine tune your script to incorporate "objection busters" is invaluable.

An example of a multiple sales call scenario where a decision must be made at a certain point in time could incorporate this example into the opening section of the script:

◊   Mr. X… Today's business is very demanding, as is our time. We're all under pressure to deliver results and I'm sure you are no different.
◊   What we do to ensure the best result for both of us is to arrange for two or three detailed meetings where we will cover all aspects of the product and your requirements. We will build a needs analysis and suitability analysis with you and we will present solutions which will be suitable for your business.

◊   At that point you will be well equipped with all the facts and figures and you will be in a position to make choices regarding what will work for you or what will not.
◊   When you reach this point I am going to ask you for a decision. As research has shown… the most powerful time to make decisions is when all the facts are clear and in front of you and the information is fresh, allowing you to make clear informed choices.
◊   This way we can both effectively manage our business while allowing us to be clear on whether we agree on a solution together or not… and that's fair to both of us isn't it?
◊   The last thing you want and the last thing I can afford is to have someone calling you every other day chasing you for a decision. That is detrimental to you and to me.
◊   So, our plan is to schedule two or three meetings, obtain all the necessary information and requirements you may have, present options, and finally to present solutions from which you can make informed decisions… that's acceptable, isn't it?
◊   So, let's schedule our next meeting… when will be suitable… Thursday the XXX or Tuesday the XXXX…..

And a direct sale approach might have this written into the script:

"Mr. X, as you would probably realise, I meet with hundreds of families such as yours. What I have learned from all these opportunities is that families and individuals such as you like to be able to make clear and informed decisions, especially when it involves their family… I'm sure you are no different.

What I have learned during this time is that the facts prove without a shadow of a doubt that research is correct when it reveals that all of us as people fail to retain nearly 90% of what we we're shown within twenty-four hours of the information being presented, once that information is taken away. That means less than 10% retention of the facts and information remains with us, after a short period of time. What this research also shows is that the best time to make a decision is when the information is fresh and right in front of you. And that makes sense, doesn't it, because you have access to everything while it is with you.

With this in mind I am going to ask you a favour....

With all these facts in place and due to the number of families I see everyday, I am going to ask you that when we are finished and I have completed my presentation and answered all your questions... and please feel free to ask as many questions as you would like... at that point I am going to ask you to make a decision. A decision that says you would like to take advantage of this service for your family... or no, you would not like to take advantage of the opportunity. With that we can all remain friends and you can be sure you are making the best decision possible while all the information is fresh and present, and that's fair to both of us, isn't it?"

You will notice a very important (it looks minor, but is actually a major point) event takes place during my request. I ask the customer to do me a favour! Now why would a customer who does not know me want to do a favour for me? Well the truth is that people feel empowered when they believe they are helping someone else. Giving the help or providing the favour as opposed to receiving the help or the favour is more powerful to the customer than the other way around. As soon as I asked customers if they would do a favour for me, they were more receptive, more favourable to oblige and agree.

Not only did I ask for a favour, and the favour was that they would agree to making a decision, but the customer now felt involved, and empowered to make this decision… and they participated with more enthusiasm and interest. They were now clear on what was going to be asked of them, and they were more determined to ensure they knew what they were going to be deciding on.

The objection disappeared!!! It actually disappeared and was never a factor again in my sales career. On the very few occasions when the customer would attempt to reinstate the "I want to think about it" objection, I would simply (kindly, and with a smile on my face) remind them that they had agreed to helping me by committing to making a decision. I would remind them again of the statistics and facts surrounding the best time to decide and then actually lead them back into the opportunity to decide what was best for them. In fact, most of the time, I would lead in with the option for them to simply say "no" by expressing to them that they were actually doing me more of a favour to just say "no" right there and then if that was the committed answer – rather than if they wanted me to call back or come back to them later as this was more difficult for me than a simple "no".

The psychology of this approach is that customers do not want to say "no" in such a direct manner, they feel as if they are hurting your feelings and would rather say "I want to think about it" because they think this is a softer let down than a direct "no". What I would do is appeal to their empathetic view of my situation… I had so many people to see, and my work took me to new locations every day. To call back would mean someone else would not be getting a chance to take advantage of the opportunity and that meant someone was losing out. So my response would go something like this:

"Mr X., I certainly appreciate your desire to do the best for your family and this is obviously an important decision for you. As we agreed earlier in the presentation, the best time to decide is when the information is fresh, in front of you and clearly presented so that you have all the facts in order to make the best decision… and you agreed that you would help me out in this regard.

I am sure you can appreciate that I see a lot of people everyday, and if I had to spend all my time going back to see all the people I had already visited, then I would never get to anyone new, as all my time would be used going back, instead of moving forward. That is why I am prepared to rather have you say "no", you would like to pass on this opportunity instead of asking me to come back or call back. The problem of course is that I can see you are very interested in the service I am offering… otherwise you would have already said "no". So with that in mind, I am more concerned with answering whatever questions you have involving the service I am offering you so that you can make a good decision rather than closing up and leaving you with questions unanswered, so please help me by asking whatever it is that is may be just a little unclear… do you have questions on the price, how you can pay for the product, or is it on how you can use the product and what the benefits are to you?"

[With that… shut up… let him tell you what the question or concern is, because he will].

From this the customer would either tell me what the questions might be or they would tell me that they had no questions… everything was clear; they just needed to talk about it. I would then answer their questions and close again by asking what option they would prefer and what payment plan they prefer.

OR…………… if they had no questions would state they just needed to talk about it… I would immediately get up, leave everything in front of them (all my materials, the agreement, the PEN) and head out the door stating almost over my shoulder – "okay then, I am going to give you 15-20 minutes to talk it over and I'll come back and get your decision then, please feel free to go through the materials and the agreement, and I will see you in a few minutes" (And out the door I would go).

I will conclude this example by saying that between the "objection buster" inserted into my presentation… the reminder if the objection was resurrected… and the action taken to leave the customer to make a decision (with all my stuff left in the house) my closure rate reached my objective – 100% decisions each time, every time! Were they always 100% in the "yes" to a sale? No, they were not, but I never did another call back, decisions were made… yes or no, and that is the objective, isn't it?

I was able to walk out of every home feeling satisfied that I had done my best; satisfied that a decision was made and it did not need to play on my mind that maybe I could have done something more to get a decision, because I was now doing just that – everything I could to ensure a decision was made.

From this method, did my positive closure rate of successful sales opportunity increase? Yes it did – dramatically, to more than 60% which needless to say for direct door to door sales was phenomenal. And more importantly, I felt confident and satisfied that I was doing the best job possible for myself and for my customers. We all finished each visit with a decision made and we could both be satisfied with that. The customer was satisfied, I was satisfied and I was able to continue forward with seeing new prospects and that is the aim. We will cover closing and objections in a bit more detail later, but I felt that insight into the process and examples relating to the process were necessary in this chapter on Process.

Next in the process chain -

FIRST IMPRESSIONS:

1. Be on time – actually you need to be five minutes early – always! This is the very first impression given – the customer will begin to judge you even before you arrive. If you arrive late or even latish to the exact minute or slightly late you will immediately be judged as not professional, not caring enough to even just be on time. Not concerned, or worse, not interested. Not excited enough about your product or company. Not confident, or arrogant, or you may be judged to be sloppy or careless. All of these thoughts can and do arise and you can be behind the 8-ball before you even begin. It also makes the customer uneasy and uncomfortable, because in their mind they have already formed an opinion and then it becomes difficult to alter this image without feeling as if they are lowering their standard or being untrue to themselves.

2. Dress professionally and smart – you should be the best dressed person in the room. Customers will always be impressed that you thought enough of them to be dressed well. It also establishes a dominant position immediately because you are the best dressed in the room. It dismisses the opportunity of you being discounted or looked down upon because of how you are dressed. Do not think that people will accept you for who you are – people respect that you value their time and treat them with respect by dressing professionally.

3.   Be firm in your handshake and greeting – again, this is the customer's first opportunity to size you up and if you come across as weak or lacking confidence it is not going to help you win them over.

OPENING - THE FIRST THREE MINUTES:

The first three minutes are crucial – customers will always remember the first impression. Be prepared for this opening three minutes to grab their attention – this is your three minutes to impress and win them over. What you present regarding your product or service in the opening, or what you present in order to gain entry or gain the appointment, has long range benefits or repercussions.

From that point forward the customer is anxious to hear what you have to say, they already are beginning to trust you, and they regard you as a professional ally, someone they can trust to help guide them.

Step 1: Open with your best and close with your second best.

1.   The reason why this principle holds true is that you have three minutes to make an impression and get the customer's attention.
2.   You have three minutes to establish that you are professional, you are there to do business and that you have something of interest for the customer to see.
3.   You must open with a powerful benefit statement or powerful benefit of the product or service, so they immediately recognise they stand to gain in this process. This is what sets the tone for the rest of your presentation and sets the tone for the closing sequence.

Step 2: Tell them your agenda and what you would like to present (once you gain entry or gain the appointment / ability to proceed).

1. Tell them what you have in store for them and how it is going to benefit them.
2. Tell them you have prepared for them an insight into who you are and what you represent – your company and your product – and tell them that your aim is to help them.
3. You are there to provide benefits which will enable them to enjoy benefits, gain something in their life or business, save time, money, resources.
4. You are there to provide benefits which will assist them in growing their business and making more money.
5. You are there to provide products or services which will enhance their life.

Step 3: Encourage interaction.

Once you have impressed them with the first three minutes, ask them approvingly if the plan is suitable for them and would they like you to continue (may I continue?). This encourages their interaction and their commitment to the process and you already have buy-in to what you would like to do. This will allow you to move on to the body of your sales process.

You might say something like this in the opening sequence – "I am here to assist you in viewing a few choice options that are designed for you to receive maximum benefit, along with that at the end of the process I will outline the few choice options you may choose from in order to take advantage of the solution. Allow me to present these options and explain the benefits of each"… and then move into the body of your sales process.

Step 4: Closing /Confirming the sale

The closing sequence must fit in with your opening statement and conclude the sale as one unified process. At the end you will be able to tie the process together neatly into a limited few neat choice options for them to select as you assist them with their decision making process (at this point they will rely on you for guidance as you are the authority and they trust that you have their best interest at heart... and obviously you do).

Let's Recap:

1. Create a script – just like an actor or a movie – know where you are going, what you want to say, how you want to say it.
2. Practice – speak it out loud, listen to yourself, practice in front of a mirror, do role-play, rehearse, re-work your script, practice some more. Learn your process word for word – know exactly where you are and where you are going every time.
3. Prepare for your sales presentations by making that GREAT first impression:
    1. Be on time – that is five minutes early
    2. Be dressed professionally (be the best-dressed in the room)
    3. Open with your best! Make that benefit statement that gets their interest!
    4. Sell benefits and find exciting benefits for them – the customer
    5. Find their 'wants' and pay attention to what interests them.
4. Tie the entire process together leading to the closing sequence where you assist the customer with their decision and confirm the sale.

OK. Now we have the preparation and process under control it's time to get to that all important moment – getting the decision! On to Chapter 5.

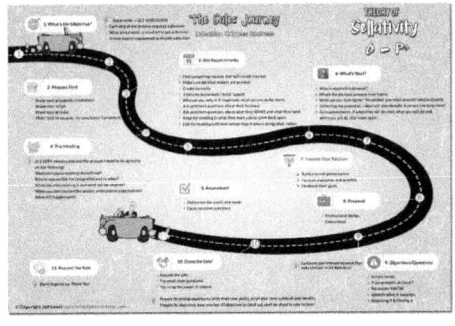

Get your beautiful FREE bonus
"Sales Journey Wall Chart"

Visit
www.sellativitysolutions.com

CHAPTER FIVE

Getting a Decision

Well, well, well, so we arrive at the destination, the objective, the desire of every professional sales person. The culmination of all that hard work, the alpha and omega of the sales process!

And what do we see? This is what has become of the sales professional, is it? Decades of sales training, centuries of business and trade, millions of stores, billions of products, thousands upon millions of opportunities every single day around the globe and today are generally accepted sales opportunity has been reduced to a 20 % sales success?

Well I would almost be embarrassed if I didn't know better and didn't know that there was an answer… a solution… a 100% guaranteed delivery plan. And the best thing about it is that it isn't five-hundred steps to success or one-hundred easy methods to learn to be good at sales, or even ten principles to achieve, etc. It is three basic fundamentals – that's it three things to do to become professional and successful. And the first one starts here:

#1 – the most dramatic, most important, most fundamental: Get A Decision!

So, you want to be a salesperson? Just why is that? Are you not interested in going to school for a 'real' job, can't find any other work (sarcasm)? Maybe you think you like working with people, and you have a nice smile and good attitude?

How many salespeople are out there in the world anyway? Think about every company, every small business, every retail shop, every business has some aspect of sales and some semblance of salespeople or someone to sell the product, service, solution, etc.

Obviously this means that there is always a sales position available somewhere, it also means there is plenty of competition by other so-called salespeople. With all these millions of competitors out there, just what is it that you are going to do differently to stand out, to be chosen first, to achieve the most success?

Any number of reasons (some even as lame as the ones above) may have led you to realise you have talent and enjoy the challenge of making that sale. Maybe you are a competitive person and have a desire to win; maybe you just enjoy the conversational relationship of talking to another person. Whatever it is, somewhere in there you decide (that's funny isn't it?) or you get maneuvered into a sales position.

So now what do you do? Run away screaming like you are being chased by wild stampeding herds of buffalo? Cry and plead for someone to release you from this fate? Cling on to the nearest resemblance of an experienced salesperson for dear life?

Well maybe what you do is get yourself educated and figure out what this game is all about. So where do you start? Well the first step is to figure out what it is that you are supposed to do. I mean, like, what is the goal, the objective, the reason you are out there in the first place? Yeah, I know, everybody will tell you the normal – "to make the sale", "to make money", "to make them say yes".

And it couldn't be easier or simpler. I am going to relieve your anxiety right now and reveal the secret, the secret that lies shrouded behind millions of closed doors and closed minds. The secret that haunts would-be salespeople every day.

An objective and achievement so simple and one that makes so much sense that everybody misses it on their way to "making that sale". It is as basic as basic can be and the foundation stone of tremendous success... and I do mean tremendous success: Get a decision, and one more time with emphasis – Get A Decision !!

Now how easy is that – yipes, even I can do that I hear you confidently spurting out of your mouth. I can see your eyes brimming with tears of joy as you exclaim that if that is what is so fundamental about this whole thing, well by gosh, even you can do that. That doesn't sound difficult at all.

What would all the fuss be about if that is all there is to it (o.k., don't get carried away now laughing, cocky and way too confident YOU). Let me just understand this again I can hear you saying "Get A Decision"... that's the big mystery, the big secret??

Yes, it absolutely is. The road to overwhelming, tremendous, fantastic, super-stardom sales success is based on one principle – get a decision, a little louder now – Get A Decision – and say it with me now: GET A DECISION!! Alright, alright, so let's regain our composure and realise what the heck we are saying here. After all, how could it be this easy and yet millions of poor slobs make a hash of trying to sell anything and everything and they cannot see this one easy objective?!

Well I did say it was a mystery didn't I? Ever wonder why a mystery is a mystery to most and yet a few solve the mystery right away? Maybe they are looking for particular clues or looking in specific areas, or looking for specific telltale signs, but the fact remains that the same clues exist for all to find. The same evidence is intact, the same facts remain and yet some solve the puzzle and others do not. Why is that?

Some say the detective has an eye for it, or they have a sixth sense, or they know where to look, or they are lucky. But the fact of the matter is that they have trained themselves to search for particular clues or circumstances. They have trained themselves to identify telltale signs and they have trained themselves to ask the right questions, and they have committed themselves to their objective of uncovering the facts and solving the mystery.

The point being that the objective is often very apparent and clearly visible and yet many do not see it. Like that 3D puzzle that you stick your nose up against and cross your eyes staring at. It's there and some see it plainly and others do not see it at all.

Even traffic lights or stop signs, especially after accidents when the person at fault swears he never saw the light… never saw the stop sign. Of course, you want to say "are you an idiot, how could you not see it, it was as plain as the nose on your face which I won't miss if I take a swing at it. The light / stop sign is sitting there right out in the open, how could you miss it?" And yet it happens all the time doesn't it?

Why? Because your mind is somewhere else. Because your attention is diverted or focused on something else. Perhaps you were so wrapped up in some other attention absorbing activity that you completely missed it.

Or perhaps you were never taught to pay attention to the signs? Perhaps you would rather ignore them? Hmmmmm, picking up on a pattern yet?

So the fact is – the objective is plain and simple: Get A Decision. Some see it, some don't. Some were never trained to look for it, some get sidetracked, some allow their concentration to be on other activity absorbing distractions, some don't believe the signs are important and they can do what they want, some want somebody else to notice the signs for them, some believe that they are so charming that even if they miss the signs they will be overlooked by the police whom they will schmooze and flirt and use their humor on.

Some will be told there is a stop sign or red light and yet be so committed to tuning the radio or checking the glove box, or adjusting the seat that they will ignore the objective and plow straight ahead with other intentions clearly in mind (Wow, another amazing analogy, eh? are you getting it yet?).

Ah yes, the objective… I seem to be repeating myself. However, I do hope the point is becoming clear. A simple and yet enormously overlooked objective is the key. Once you are able to recognize that the whole point of a sales call or sale presentation is to "get a decision', then all other pieces of the puzzle which make up the process all fit into place. This is the objective of every single sales call that will ever be made.

THE objective of every single sales presentation, every consulting opportunity, every suitability analysis, every needs analysis, every telesales call, every negotiation, and every sales opportunity ever presented on the face of the planet!

Every time there is a sales opportunity or deal to be made, or agreement to be reached or presentation presented means that there is an objective: Get A Decision.

Remember in our last chapter my story of how I went away from every sales call with A decision. Not a "maybe", or a "I need time" or "I'll think about it". Even if I did get a FEW "no" decisions - I still got a decision. In this chapter I really want to explore that exact part of the process in much more detail.

Now that we know it is so simple, why is it that on average 8 out of 10... 80 out of 100... 800 out of 1000, 8000 out of 10,000 (you probably follow this trend, eh?)... 80% of the time the sales process ends with NO decision? What?? Incredulous you say, let me repeat myself – umghhumph *clearing my throat* – 80% of all sales opportunities end with no request for a decision, no decision being taken, no decision asked for, no decision promised; no decision.

Well how deflating and demoralising is that? What was that all about? Clodding around for hours, days, weeks, months, and no decision came from it? What were you thinking man? Aren't you just so shocked right now that you don't know what to say?

So how does this happen, how can someone invest so much of their time and spend so much energy going through all the motions and doing all the presentations, and telling the customer so many times about how great you (the salesperson) are and how great your product and services are and then NO DECISION ??!! (run on sentence, yes I know, but it was for impact).

I can see you now with book in hand, clenching your fists and wanting to lash out at this pinhead that could be so stupid as to not 'get a decision'. Just who is this derelict of duty, this sun-dried raisin brained numbskull?! Why it's you isn't, Joe S. Salesperson?... eight out of every ten salespeople is who it is, and that my friend is sadder than sad.

All this knowledge today, all these skills, all this education, all this training, all these books and tapes and motivational courses, and seven laws of this, and eight easy steps to that, and ten habits of nuns, and five sure-fire steps to success, and twenty-one days to invincibility, and (oh that's enough isn't it?) yet what happens?

You guessed it – 800,000 times out of 1,000,000 Joe S. Salesperson is not going to ask for a decision. 800,000 times out of 1,000,000 the customer is going to say "I'd like to think about it" and walk away... never to make a decision. And what are you, Joe S. Salesperson going to do?

Nothing... That's right, let them walk away, 800,000 times out of 1,000,000. Much easier this way, and of course you will convince yourself that they mustn't make a decision too quickly, they must go away and ponder all the information and facts and one of these days that customer will magically phone you and hand over the sale. Well aren't you just the salesperson of the year! What a swell job you have done of nothing.

And another even more magical event is when the salesperson in question, Joe S. Salesperson, never even attempts to ask for a decision and yet one out of ten customers may just decide on their own with no help from you that they want to purchase what you have to sell.

And what does that mean? What does that do? That means in all actuality, that the customer himself really makes his own sale at least one out of ten times. So that means that Joe S. Salesperson is only really closing one out of ten opportunities.

What does this do to the sales profession, to the sales person, to the business?

It kills you, it kills the profession, and it creates an atmosphere of substandard acceptance, that's what it does. Slowly but surely it kills the success of a salesperson. It creates the phenomenon that is today's 80% non-decision process. And it is the salesperson's creation. Salespeople have created this monster and only salespeople are going to fix it.

This gives the sales profession such a bad name and creates such a bad taste. It creates the environment where 20% success based on the customer doing the work results in what is today deemed a successful sales proficiency.

That 20% sales success today is the general accepted sales percentage and I would stick my neck out to suggest that in no other profession would a 20% success proficiency result be rewarded with commission and incentives, let alone be deemed acceptable and merit for continuing in the position.

Imagine that you go to university for four years, six years, eight years and then write exams, pass them, graduate and then enter an intern program or apprentice program or junior position in a hospital, clinic, dental practice, law firm, brokerage company, school, engineering firm etc.

The intern program can be one to several years and then more exams are taken and the practical knowledge is tested and then and only then can you enter into the working world or doctor's practice or law firm or engineering company or accountancy practice, etc. The process is long and testing – years of schooling, endless exams, intern and apprentice programs and then when you begin work, do you get hired into the top senior position or start lower down and work your way up through proving your merits and your worth ? I think we all know the answer to this one... you must begin and then grow and climb the ladder of success.

So imagine you did all this and then started your own practice for medicine or law, or accountancy or engineering or any of these professions... and here comes Mr. Customer into your accountancy firm and they want you to handle their books and they ask you for reference or for background on your successes. At this point, because you are an honest guy, you share with the customer that you are committed to getting their books right 20% of the time, and you are sure you will guide them in all aspects of accounting for their tax requirements at least 30% of the time!

Or even better, you never tell the customer anything and then proceed to manage their account with 30% accuracy and they get hit with a whacking great audit. How happy do you think the client will be with your services?

Or Mr. Patient walks into your surgery and you explain to him that you are 40% successful on this particular operation – how comfortable or confident in your abilities do you think the patient will be? Do you think they will authorise you to perform the surgery? And if you perform the surgery and fail, do you not expect to be hearing from their attorney for malpractice at such a high failure rate and result?

And your attorney is only able to produce satisfactory results 20% of the time, would this be your top choice of attorney? The list goes on and on... an engineer who predicts even 70% success on the latest bridge being erected – would lives be given to chance? I think not. What about a stock broker or financial analyst or investor – they inform you that they achieve success on 40% of their deals – will this inspire you to invest with them?

What about a teacher teaching your children and the teacher is only teaching correct information 60% of the time – are you going to be very pleased when you realise that your children are being taught 40% wrong or incorrect information? How much will that affect their future success towards their careers?

The point is that no customer will accept less than near perfection when it comes to their well-being. They are not likely to choose inferior service or productivity in any aspect of their life, health, work, safety, etc., nor should they.

Today's marketplace enables choice and promotes productivity and winning results – why would you choose differently.

So why is it different for sales professionals? Why are they allowed to achieve success 20% of the time... 40% of the time – even 50% of the time? Why is this acceptable? I'll tell you why – because we have conditioned salespeople to believe this. Because there is no university of sales, because there are no exams, because there is no intern program or apprenticeship!
Because no-one expects a salesperson to achieve better? Because the salesperson thinks he is performing wonderfully at 20, 30, 40 %?

Well I do not accept it!

Pride and desire to be a professional should drive you to study, research, investigate, practice, undergo exams, practice, perform practical exercises, study some more, practice some more and perfect your methods! Am I right?! Yes! We expect this from all professions don't we? They must practice and practice until they know what they are doing every time – yes?

Every single time… we do not accept that this time they were unprepared do we? We expect them to get it right every time – and why not sales? Do you think it is because we have become so accustomed to every Tom, Dick & Harry being a salesperson that we just accept that most of them are not very good at it?

Do we build businesses that accommodate paying lower salaries and providing sales commissions on sales achievements of 20%, AND that we drive a mentality of needing more salespeople at these accepted levels of success in order for us to achieve our company goals? Did you get that?

Companies think because success is figured into their budgets based on 20% achievement that what they need are more salespeople.

Five salespeople at 20% equals 100% of my requirements for my business – isn't that logical? That is how business operates, isn't it? If Joe S. Salesperson gets 20%, then four more Joe's will get me what I need – except that now I have the expense of five Joe's instead of one, so the budget requirements keep going up.

I believe that we encourage and create these environments and these accepted parameters, because I have witnessed it around the world for the last 25 years. More and more I see so-called 'salespeople' abusing this trend and the majority of them are no more a salesperson than they are a brain surgeon. Yet we continue to perpetuate the myth that they are salespeople because they look nice, smile nice, have a nice personality, sell at 20% closing ratio and are fun people to be around. So what happened to qualified quality sales professionals?

Oh, they're out there, but they are becoming rare only because I believe no attention is being paid to the profession and I intend to change that. When you deal with a sales professional, you should expect 100% effort and performance, just as you would from a surgeon. Sales professionals must be capable of 'Getting A Decision'

at least 90% of the time and should strive for 100% results every time, just as a surgeon, or accountant, or engineer would do. We all realise that no-one is perfect and even the best surgeons can sometimes not perform to the highest proficiency, yet they can be sure of following the proper procedure and process every time and that is what sales professionals must also learn to do. If sales professionals follow the process and rely on this #1 golden rule they can achieve results every single time they meet with a customer. It all starts with this easy, simple, effective, common sense rule: Ask for a decision, and more importantly – get a decision!!

Once you realise that all sales starts and ends with a simple rule of getting a decision, the obvious next step is just how to go about 'getting this decision'.

The initial work begins between your ears, thinking and realising what needs to occur in every sales opportunity, and believe me when I say "Every opportunity in business is a sales opportunity". Someone is being sold. Did you get this? Either you as the salesperson are being sold on the reason why they, the buyer, doesn't want to decide right now, or needs more time, or wants to think it over, or whatever other reason is being offered as to why they will not decide now... or... you as the salesperson is selling the reason why the buyer needs and wants to make a decision now. Every opportunity in business results in a sale of some type, the salesperson sells his product or service or the buyer sells his reasons why he cannot purchase the product or service.

The danger is when the sale made is the one where no decision is made. This sale results in all parties being dissatisfied and frustrated. Not sure that this is true? Try this example and insight: Indecision is the greatest crippler of business. Indecision will cripple your business and eventually put you out of business. Indecision is a killer! And not just for you the salesperson who is anxiously awaiting this sale, but for the business owner / buyer / decision maker who stifles his own business when he sits with indecision.

Many times the buyer / business owner / decision maker does not realise that this phenomenon is taking place and will actually state that they have so many offers to consider that they are having a hard time making a decision. So what happens is that nothing happens and it festers and clouds the judgment of the buyer toward any further decisions which need taken in their process. They often don't realise this is taking place until too many issues come to climax and the buyer makes snap decisions because he can no longer cope with the many issues on his desk.

Generally this results in little creative growth as the easiest decision is to decide to do nothing – cancel everything, go back to basics and sit tight. When too many decisions pile up this is generally the release – say no to everything and continue as standard. Only when business really begins to decline do business owners / buyers / decision makers then realise they need to do something and then call in the salespeople again to assess a few options and the choices start again.

Now the professional salesperson will discover this in their 'sellativity' process, asking pertinent questions about their background, why the business owner is now investigating options, what desired outcome is expected, what expectations the business owner has on the products or services you are presenting, and when the business owner would expect to take action. These are all fact finding and decision making questions designed to prime the pump for the final requests for a decision, for which the decision maker will be ready for because he has been outlining all the reasons why he needs to make decisions now in his business.

When no decision is made there exists an environment of unsurety (new word), uncertainty, and indecisiveness. A lack of clear direction, an uncertainty of whether to proceed or not. A fork in the road and unsurety as to whether to proceed left or right… so what happens?

You sit there in the fork in the road trying to determine which way to go, fearful of making the wrong choice. Fearful of not making the best decision, and what happens? What happens is that the simple act of not deciding is actually the decision itself and this starts eroding your options and opportunities because while you are sitting there waiting to decide, choice opportunities on either road are not coming your way. You miss the opportunities on either road because you are sitting back at the fork in the road trying to decide. You end up with no options and no opportunities, all because you were uncertain and wanted to ensure you made the best decision.

Fear of making the wrong decision or of just not making the best decision can cause you more harm than actually making a wrong decision and quickly realising that it is not the best decision and then correcting it and getting back on the right road to success.

Rather to be progressing on a road to somewhere where you are able to judge and measure results pertaining to making this choice and choosing this road, than to make no choice and not be able to measure or judge either road's success or failures. Fear of making the right choice (or wrong choice…

I choose to stay on the positive side of fear of success as opposed to fear of failure) can be scary and full of anxiety and concerns. However, fear from making a choice and allowing that fear to become the deciding factor is a killer for your business and your life. When you choose to remain outside the game and just be an observer means that you are never a participant in the game, never a player, only an observer. And the longer range view to this fence-sitting is that once you choose nothing – when you choose not to make a choice – you effectively eliminate all opportunities which would be available on either road that you did not travel.

You will recognise in business today that the businesses driven by decision makers are the ones growing and thriving and evolving all the time.

They must stay ahead of the curve and maintain their position in the market. They will not achieve this by sitting back and doing nothing or choosing nothing. They cannot stand pat and achieve growth results. What they will have is a stagnating business which continues to hang on by their fingertips, trusting that the market will change or the customer will remain loyal.

When you dig into these businesses, you realise they feel they are in a strong position and want to remain very cautious and conservative regarding any new decisions or evolution of their business. They research endlessly, conduct polls, run surveys, petition their staff and in the end they are still left grappling with inconclusive data and reliant on their own decision making abilities.

Those that make decisions and proceed are able to guide their own ship through whatever waters they encounter, be it smooth sailing or stormy seas – they are still in control of their ship as they know where they are heading. But the ship that is left to the mercy of the sea is in danger of being ripped apart by the elements as it is drifting on the currents as opposed to being driven to its destination.

The point is that all buyers want to decide once they understand the dynamics of what happens when they don't decide. It becomes your job to set the foundation and assist the buyer in the decision making process. Once that buyer realises that it is in his best interests to make a decision he will never again be left to delaying decisions which are important to his progress. Your job is to assist, to allay those fears, to understand those concerns, to generate clear and concise choices, to build the confidence of the buyer in your knowledge and expertise.

To create an environment where the buyer is comfortable, secure and confident in his ability to make a choice – to make a decision. The ability to create this setting is 'Sellativity'.

Any buyer will be more satisfied realising that they have made a clear, concise and educated decision based on the facts and information. This allows them to move on to their next item of business with a clear conscience and a clear mind, ready for the next challenge. When there are consistently and constantly issues hanging over their head they are not able to concentrate fully on the task at hand. All issues have a domino affect, with realisation that each decision could impact or have effect upon the other issue that you have not yet reached a decision on. Each of these non-decisions impacts the business on a growing scale as each issue impacts the next with staggering results. Slowly the business grinds to a halt because no decisions can be made moving forward until fundamental decisions are established and set in place.

Therefore, when decision makers are able to make clear decisions it takes the monkey off their back and allows them the freedom to move forward making new decisions on new opportunities based on previous decisions already in place. One foundation establishes the opportunity for growth and evolution in a business.

Most importantly – decision makers like to be able to get on with their business at hand and need clear views in order to be in position to take advantage of the initiatives planned. When decisions are made confidently and with surety the business can surge forward. And finally Business Owners and decision makers like to be congratulated and commended for making good choices and good decisions, so help them with that desire.

So we started off in the beginning of this chapter establishing that the fundamental initial phase of the process starts between your ears – thinking and planning. Thinking of what the situation involves, the background, the circumstances, the expectations and the process. How will you progress, what will you ask, what information is required, when will they want to act, who will be involved, why will they consider your offer and proposal, etc. You must plan what you are going to do, and be prepared when you are presented with your opportunity.

So how do you prepare the buyer for making a decision?

Let's consider building a platform for your presentation, one where you can be assured the customer will make a decision based on your assistance. First we must build the foundation... what if we tried something like this as an introduction :

"Mr. Customer, I am sure you would agree that time is valuable and we all get numerous pressures on our time. Opportunities to evaluate solutions are precious time options and require that we utilise them fully in order to take advantage of such opportunities. Therefore, I am here to assist you in recognising benefits of our solutions which will boost your business to new levels and productivity, giving you an advantage in the marketplace and allowing you more time to build and grow your business as you desire.

As I am sure you are qualified and possess the expertise required to run your business, I am also qualified and posses the expertise required to assist you with any and all questions you may have regarding our solution and that is why I am here.

One thing we have learned in today's society is that information is vital in making solid decisions and choices.

Research has shown that 40-50% of the information we receive in a presentation will be forgotten within two to three hours, a further 10-20% forgotten within twenty-four hours; up to 90% will be forgotten within forty-eight to seventy-two hours after we're presented with this information.

That is why cramming for exams has always been a practice for exams. However, what research has also shown is that decisions are made most clearly and accurately when the information is fresh at hand and fresh in the mind of the person making the decision.

That is why I am here to assist you and I am going to ask you one small favour which is for your benefit if I may? (Pause for effect and to allow confirmation).

Because all the research points to the fact that decisions are best made when the information is fresh in front of you, I am going to ask that in order to allow us both to perform at our highest level and in order for you to receive the greatest benefit… that when I am finished and have been able to answer all your questions and supplied you with all the information that you require to make a sound, clear decision, that when we arrive at this time that you are able to say to me "Yes, you would like to take advantage of our solution or No, that you wouldn't" and that's fair isn't it? (pause and wait for his answer).

This permits us both to manage our time which is valuable and allows us both to have a clear conscience and clear thought process for the continuance of our business – yes?"

What have you done?

You have effectively removed the objection which could come later when the customer says to you that they want to think about it, consider the options, go through the materials and make up their mind, liaise with other others for their opinion, etc. The customer has now effectively confirmed with you that he will make a decision once you guide him through the solution offer.

Even if your sales process involves more than one visit or meeting, you can get a decision each time to continue with the next meeting and the same rule will apply… when you are done, you will ask the customer for "yes, they would like to take advantage of your solution or No, they wouldn't".

This method allows you to manage and control your business. It also allows you to understand why the customer may not choose your solution offer, because if they say no, you are going to ask them politely "why" (more on this in chapter Ten).

It allows you to continue on with your sales prospects and not get hung up on always chasing the ones who are 'thinking it over' or 'considering the options' or 'talking with colleagues' or any number of other non-decision making practices.

Remember when I said to you that in-decision kills your business – think about this… when you are constantly chasing old customers who have not yet made up their mind, how do you have any time to see new prospective customers? Do you realise how deadly the practice is of phoning back old customers to constantly chase them regarding their choice?

The information has faded from their memory and the only thing they see now is you calling to pester them and chase them. Do you think this is endearing to the customer? Do you think they cannot wait to receive your phone call? Or do they say they will call you and sit forever waiting for this magical call?

Indecision cripples you in another way as well. When you allow a customer to say he will phone you when he has decided and then miraculously one phones one day, what do you think this does to your thought process? You begin to think this is an accepted proactive and start to rely on this happening with every other customer who tells you this. Slowly you have all customers promising to phone you and for every one out of one-hundred who does phone you, you have lost the other ninety-nine. This is what creates the statistics that we see represented today in the accepted sales world. Sales people not designing a process to manage the decision making process – deadly, killing, crippling.

I must tell you here that this process of laying the foundation for getting a decision was based on a hand-to-mouth experience. Excuse me… What? A hand-to mouth experience? What is that, a sales procedure? Well actually, no. It is a 'sellativity' experience which actually means that if I didn't figure out a way to overcome this particular objection and roadblock early in my sales career, I was soon going to have no food moving between my hand and mouth!

As it was at this time, I was doing as many sales demos or sales presentations per day as humanly possible. Our Sales Director sent our guidelines that said twenty-seven sales demos per week would generally (average across the territory) result in five to six sales per week or approximately 20-22% which was our region average.

Now each demo took approximately sixty to ninety minutes and then another fifteen to twenty minutes of overcoming objections, so it was quite exhausting to do five to six of these per day. And to make things really interesting, five to six sales per week was absolutely minimum requirement for me to live and pay my bills. Due to financing of the deals, commission hold back percentage due to customer repayment schemes, taxes, medical aid, etc. the money received from these sales barely covered all the responsibilities and still allowed for me to eat.

So a few things became very clear once I found my feet and realised that I did have the ability to get in the door, present a demo and ask for the order.

What were they?

Number 1 – I figured out that the presentation was too long and had to get their attention sooner and close sooner, so I began work on that aspect of the presentation.

Number 2 – I was doing a great job creating interest and asking for the order.

Number 3 – I was constantly and consistently being faced with the fact that after all this effort and asking for the order, the customer insisted on a period of time to "think about it". Ugh... after all that effort I was constantly being hit with this objection and I would do my job of asking what it was they would like to consider, how I could help answer their questions, what questions did they still have, how I could assist them with their decision making process, and was there something I missed that had left them with concerns or doubts?

(All these by the way are great antidotes to the "think about it" objection and I will deal with these in more detail in Chapter 10) but more often than not, I would leave the home without the order and with a request to follow up with them later when they had time to think it over.

95% of these never amounted to a sale and the very few that did actually did more harm for me than good as it created false hope and the illusion that customers would follow though later with an order. What also occurred with these follow ups were time wasting phone calls and drive-backs and endless chasing until the customer and/or myself became exhausted with the process of continual call-backs and the process slowly eroded into the pit of "think-about-it" prospects that never result in a sale.

So what did I do?

I built a process to overcome this – scripted into the opening scenes of the demo – designed to eliminate this objection and create an environment of decisions making paradise that would allow my customers and myself to feel good about our meeting together and feel confident that we had both accomplished our objective – getting a decision! I outlined that part of the process in the previous chapter – where I changed my script
after recording as much of the sales process as possible after every single demo and then altered my script to include these objections.

Remember how many times this worked? Every time – should I say it again – every time! My dilemma of "think-about-it" was gone! What did it do to my sales – shot through the roof.

My ability to CLOSE a sale and get on to the next customer relieved me of call backs, chasing endlessly for no decision and allowed me to concentrate fully on the next prospect which allowed me to continue to assess and analyse my process and recognise the next objection that became redundant and needed attention.

I will cover more of these as we continue as there is always another objection or concern to be dealt with (and we shall deal with them). My successful "yes" closing percentage went from 20 to 40 to 60% within weeks of discovering and dealing with this particular objection. Would it go higher??? Wait and see.

I want to complete this chapter with this thought - If every profession on the planet requires a process and procedure to ensure success in their respective profession, why not sales? Why not design a process which will eliminate an objection before you get to the end of a presentation? Especially an objection which is the kingpin, the mainstay, the killer of all sales presentations?

The delayed decision, the "think-about-it", the "talk-it- over", the "need-some-time" objection is the derailer of thousands of sales opportunities – millions of sales opportunities. And the sad part is that the customer is the one who suffers. The customer who has unwittingly invited indecision into his business.

The customer who unknowingly has placed his company or his business at an impasse. The customer becomes a risk to his own business and his own well-being because the salesperson is not doing his job professionally. It is our fault when we do a disservice to our customers by not assisting them with making a decision.

Remember the opening chapters – 80% of salespeople never ask for a decision – never ask for the order – never ask for the sale. They just blast away with their machine gun of sales information and hope that a few bullets hit their target and the customer will succumb to the onslaught and ask the salesperson to sign them up.

Because they have never been taught how to ask for a decision, they do not realise that there is a better way. An easier way! So let's start making use of this easier way, this process of building a foundation to make decision making simpler, better, more effective.

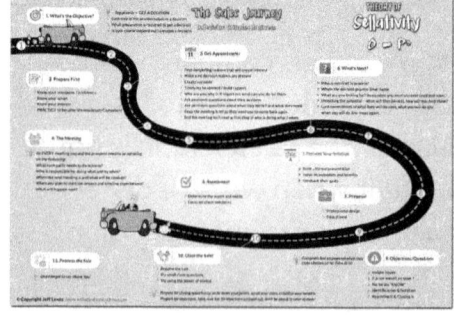

Get your beautiful FREE bonus
"Sales Journey Wall Chart"

Visit
www.sellativitysolutions.com

CHAPTER SIX

Unconsciously Incompetent

Now that we have the principle elements of what will help you set the scene for success, let's examine this core fundamental process – the process that everyone goes through, sometimes without even realising that they are navigating through a process...

Have you ever heard of this progressive axiom?

1. Unconsciously incompetent
2. Consciously incompetent
3. Consciously competent
4. Unconsciously competent

Here is how this process works and what it means for you:

1. Unconsciously incompetent – you don't know that you don't know. Before you looked into space for the first time or considered a sales career for the first time, you don't know what you do not know. Think about any new venture that you discover – before you enter into this venture, you are not even aware of the things that you know nothing about. Space, stars, the galaxy, constellations... until you get interested and look up into the sky, you are not even aware that there are planets and clusters and constellations, and galaxies out there. You know nothing about it. You are unconsciously incompetent to discuss any aspects of this sky above your head. In effect, you do not even know that you do not know anything about it. It has never entered your sphere of thinking or your thoughts. It is an aspect that is not in your knowledge. Sales is the same – until you begin, you do not even realise that there are aspects of the profession that you know nothing about – you are therefore unconsciously incompetent.

You cannot speak with authority on any aspect of the process because you did not even know there was a process.

2.   Consciously incompetent – you now know that you do not know... now you look into space and realise there are tons of stars up there and you do not know what they are. Are they planets in our solar system, stars, clusters, galaxies, solar system, Milky Way? So you are looking at them and you realise that you want to know what they are, where they are, how far away they are, what their names are, how old they are... you now realise that you know that you do not know anything about them and you want to know. Sales is the same – so you look at this profession now and realise there is more to this than you thought, because previously you were not aware of what was involved – you were unconsciously incompetent. Now you become consciously incompetent – you realise that there are things you want to know and must now take action to learn about them.

3.   Consciously competent – you begin to learn and apply what you learn... now you take your star guidebook with you and you study the stars and the sky and the galaxy. When you look up into the sky you have your book with you and you refer to the stars in the sky as represented in the book and you learn where they are and how far and what their names are. With effort and assistance you begin to consciously know what you are talking about. You become consciously competent. It takes effort but you start to learn and utilise the knowledge in your understanding of the night sky.

The sales profession is the same – you begin to learn and with assistance you apply the knowledge you learn to practical examples and you become able to apply process and procedure to sales opportunities. As you learn and remember and apply the knowledge learned you become consciously competent. You become able to think about a particular example and apply the reasoning behind it to arrive at a conclusion and solution. With thinking and effort you become consciously competent.

4.   Unconsciously competent – you now apply the lessons learned almost automatically… you become so adept and knowledgeable on the subject that you have the information at your fingertips. You now gaze up at the night sky and you know where the constellations are, you know which is which, how far away they are, which ones are planets, clusters, galaxies, etc. Sales becomes the same – you begin to know by memory how to process a situation, what lessons to apply, how to proceed, what to say, how to ask the question, etc. You become proficient in assisting the customer to utilise the information provided in order to reach a conclusion and make a decision. You become unconsciously competent.

It becomes like learning to drive a car – a stick shift. At first it is daunting; you don't know what to expect, but you see everybody driving so it can't be too hard (at least that is what you think until you try it for the first time). You are unaware of the requirements, the process, the rules and the intricacies of clutch in, foot off accelerator, clutch slowly eased out, foot onto the accelerator, etc.

So you go through the competence process… you don't know that you don't know, then you become aware of what you don't know, then you practice and learn and sputter and stall and herk and jerk and slowly but surely get the hang of it (consciously competent) and then over time and practice you become oblivious to what is required as you motor down the road, talking to friends, singing to the tunes on the radio… clutch in, clutch out, change gears, accelerate, smooth and slick as you head on down the road, not even concerned or thinking about what is required to make the car go.

How competent you have become without giving it a single thought or worry – what a change from a few months back when the thought of all the processes scared you to death.

This same process occurs with sales – learning the process, becoming aware of what is required, studying, practicing and accomplishing your goals. It follows the same process as one, two, three – as simple as that. The problem occurs when salespeople (not sales professionals) overestimate their own skills or knowledge and believe they can jump straight from step one to step ten and launch their sales career with bad habits, bad practices and bad form.

That is why this book is for you – the process is easy and simple – it outlines the steps, has very few processes or main points to learn and provides the solid foundation you need to launch your professional sales career. For me, this book is a culmination of years of selling, training, consulting, managing, directing, growing, learning, building, traveling, experiencing multi-industry cultures and most of all – discovering!

Discovering how people work, discovering what people want, discovering who I am, discovering what works and what doesn't, discovering the importance of treating people with respect and value, discovering there is a huge world out there and yet small enough to meet thousands of people and have an impact in their lives.

Discovering that helping others achieve their goals is the most exciting of all discoveries.

So the beginning point is to realise that at some point in this discovery process, you realised that you didn't know that you didn't know about sales (perhaps this is now as you contemplate a sales career), but now you do know that you at least don't know (since you are this far into the process already), therefore you are on your way to knowing now that you don't know and taking appropriate steps to ensure that you do begin to know and will soon be on the road to consciously competent selling! (whew) And if you are even a little bit confused by this last paragraph, please will you read this last bit again to ensure you "know" what we are talking about.

Now with this new knowledge on going from "Unconsciously incompetent" to "unconsciously competent" – let's move on to a big one in "sellativity": SELLING POINTS.

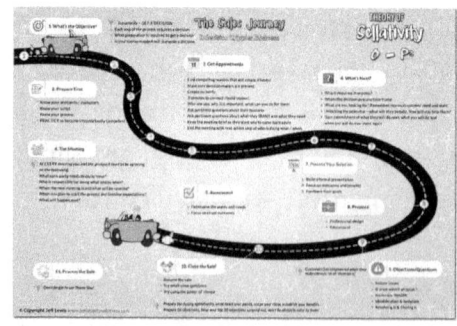

Get your beautiful FREE bonus
"Sales Journey Wall Chart"

Visit
www.sellativitysolutions.com

CHAPTER SEVEN

Selling Points

FEATURES AND BENEFITS or FEATURES Vs BENEFITS

In all sales presentations, customers are going to be attracted and interested in your solution if it not only addresses the needs of the customer, but it addresses the 'wants' of the customer as well. That is why it is important to sell according to BENEFITS because this is where you will see the excitement and interest in the customer. Those little things that makes the product fun, or easy to use, or handy, or efficient, or enjoyable to use. A source of pride is another on this list – customers love to feel pride in their new product or service, whatever it might be. Their new car, their new computer, their new cell phone, their new business system. They want to point with pride and show you all the great things it can do, and what benefits they are receiving from making such a great decision.

Magic words there – did you catch them? Benefits they receive from making such a great decision… hmmm. Pride, happiness, feeling of achievement all come with making good decisions.

Benefits vs. features – what is the difference, is there a difference? Test yourself here and explain the difference to yourself – what is a benefit and what is a feature? It is not unusual to not be able to clearly explain the difference; society and salespeople have mixed and matched these entities as if they are interchangeable. Salespeople (notice I am not saying sales professionals) have relied so heavily on a barrage of feature listing in their attempt to batter customers into submission and this has caused huge confusion. Allow me to explain and provide a simple test along with it so you will never be confused again.

a. Feature – it is something the product has or does
b. Benefit – what the result is of the feature when USED BY THE CUSTOMER

Let's look at a car's features and benefits to illustrate the differences:

Air conditioning: – feature or benefit?
Feature of course!
Feature: it is something the car has… it is a feature of the car.
What does it do? It cools the air so that the customer benefits from cool air, thereby keeping him cool and comfortable.
Benefit: keeps the customer cool and comfortable.

Air bags – feature or benefit?
Feature; of course, it is something the car has or does.
What do air bags do? They protect the customer in the case of an accident, preventing the customer from injuring themselves during impact collisions.

Feature: air bags.
Benefit: protection and safety.

Electric door locks or electric windows – feature or benefit?
Feature; of course, it is something the car has or does.
What do electric locks or windows do? They allow customers to open the door locks or windows without having to manually reach and lock or roll down windows.
Feature: electric door locks / windows.
Benefit: ease and comfort of managing doors and windows.

Here is the key: Features are what the product has or does. Benefits are what they do for you, the customer. Benefits are what you gain from using the product.

The test is a simple test. It is called the "so what" test. When presented with a question of whether the sales person is rattling off a feature list or discussing benefits with you – ask yourself or the salesperson if you want some fun – "so what" and see what results from the test.

So the car salesman is listing off his amazing features – electric windows, air conditioning, abs brakes, air bags… whoa… "So what" needs to be the question here? Is the salesperson just spewing out a feature list or is he relating it to your needs and wants? When you say "so what?", what answer do you get? Air conditioning – so what? Well the "so what" leads you to the benefit… so what – so you get a cool and comfortable environment while driving, this will help you stay cool and calm and arrive at your destination fresh and feeling good, not tired and fatigued and sweating like some kind of farm animal!

Now you have a sales benefit – a selling point to use with your presentation, not just a feature list upon which you have no idea whether the customer sees benefit or not. With feature lists you are just shooting aimlessly. With benefits, you can direct the benefit to the customer and ask them if this would benefit them and make them happy to take advantage of that particular benefit. When you sell based on benefits you are able to home in on what is exciting and interesting for a customer and what isn't. You are able to establish what selling benefits are wanted by the customer and this helps you gauge their level of interest as well as gauge their level of purchase interest.

Never underestimate what benefits are desired by a customer. Features that produce benefits that make the customer desire the product are invaluable and not to be belittled or overlooked. Why this is, is coming up in point 3, so stick with us. Benefits are the key points to be tying your presentation together. Benefits become the glue of your entire presentation and the body of your sales process.

Everything you discuss should be leading the customer to a benefit – what they will achieve by using your product. What they will gain, or what they will save (such as time and money – these always are great motivators), who will benefit from these great features, when they will benefit from them (immediately, of course), where they will be able to see the results of these benefits (in the profits, on the balance sheet, in their reports, in their life!).

These benefit statements become the lifeblood of the process – creating energy and excitement. Creating a level of desire in the customer – getting their thoughts racing, creating curiosity, and driving them to WANTING this product!

NEEDS VS. WANTS

Needs vs. wants – is there a difference, and if so, which one holds the upper hand?

You often hear of needs analysis and salespeople (not sales professionals) often talk about discovering what the customers 'needs' are. They think – salespeople that is – that if they can discover what the customer needs they can then list all their cool features related to the need and the customer will hand over the money.

I see it all the time, but sadly this method is often not successful – why?

There is a human trait that holds sway – and that is one of 'want'. Customers buy what they want. Think about it. Yes, you may need a refrigerator, but when it comes down to it, if sold properly with understanding of benefits, cool features and appeal, you will buy the one you want, more than just the one you need. Often the basic will do the trick, however… because this one does so many cool things for me, I want this one, not that basic one.

The point being, customers of course want to address needs, which is what starts them on the path of wanting to buy something anyway – they need it… for whatever reason… or so you tell yourself. Think about most 'things' we have in life. They are not absolute basic necessities like food or water – they are things we want. Our thought process convinces us that we "need" this new TV or this new car, or sofa, or microwave, or computer, or laptop, or new software application, etc. etc. etc.

The truth is the majority of what we buy or invest in is because of 'want', and there is nothing wrong with that! If we want a new software system because it will make work easier and more efficient, then that is a good thing and ensures our business is run more efficiently and skillfully. All very valid and useful benefits – but don't lose sight of the fact that your business could run on paper systems if required and it would mean more work and more time expended and more possibility of errors, but nevertheless, it would work if we "needed" it to.

STORY STORY STORY

I think it is here that I will share one story which just shows how much fun you can have when you do not let situations intimidate you.

I had been training a new guy, which always involved training them on how to achieve success by cold calling door-to-door, because the reality was that if you could achieve success there, you could achieve success anywhere. Managing leads and prospecting and referrals and all the other sales related activities became cake once you could manage door-to-door. So anyway, I was training the new guy, we'll call him Bob, and Bob was looking a bit overwhelmed and intimidated by some of the responses we were getting at the doors of the homes we were visiting when all of a sudden the next house became an adventure of note.

I was trying to get Bob to try his luck and he kept on insisting that I just needed to show him a couple more so he could get it down pat. His time was running out, but I accepted that I would handle a couple more while he worked up his courage. While discussing the next strategy, I knocked on the next door – boom boom boom, came the thuds of footsteps approaching the door, it sounded like a gorilla approaching, wham the door flew open and slammed against the inside wall – "what the hell do you want" spewed the woman at the door, hair in a frenzy, nostrils flaring and I am sure I saw fire belching from her throat as she defied us to say another word!!! She bellowed again – "get the hell out of here and don't bother me with any of your crap" and slammed the door shut before we had a chance to swallow (which was tough to do because we were scared out of our wits). I took one look at Bob and knew his career had just ended unless I could think fast and take action. It hit me like an epiphany and I grabbed Bob and quickly said – We're heading for the back door – with a huge smile on my face. Bob's look was incredible… he swallowed hard, tried to get his legs to follow my pull on his arm and stammered out "are you nuts, she's going to kill us if we bother her again". I said – "c'mon Bob, she's going to love it" and raced for the back door which you can do in middle America because there are no walls or fences, or barricades.

So we ran to the back and I quickly knocked again quite forcefully on the back door and prepared for the fire breathing action figure to reappear. Well appear she did, with stomping and cursing and vengeance headed for the door from inside. Bob tensed and prepared for his life to end and the door ripped open and nearly came off the hinges – but this time – before a word could come out of her mouth I rattled off – "Man, I hope you're not as nasty as that woman we met at the front door, wow was she mad!" and offered a huge grin. Well, that did it, she couldn't do anything but grin, then smile then laugh… she laughed so hard she invited us in.

She thought that was the most audacious and funny thing she had ever witnessed in her life and couldn't help but laugh. She then broke down and told us how she had been having the most horrendous morning and how everything had been going wrong and then we showed up at just the worst time and how atrocious she acted and would we forgive her, and on and on. What she needed was someone to listen to her and we did that, and she also bought some of our materials that she thought would be helpful for her grandchildren who were part of the morning's heated moments. It appeared that their mother – our new friend's daughter – was not managing her role very well as mother and that was part of the problem.

Nevertheless, the point is – every situation creates its own opportunities if you recognise them and take advantage of them. Events do not happen by coincidence – they happen for a reason if we are just prepared to act on them.

Lesson: Bob learned that any situation could be managed and every situation was an opportunity if he just followed through and didn't shrug it off. He learned to not be intimidated by anything and, more importantly, Bob learned to persevere and think on his feet. He learned that he could actually get through just about any incident and went on to great success and was one of my top guys, and I believe all because of this opportunity.

So – we have our process, our objections are under control, we have mastered our selling pints and tamed the crankiest customer. What now? It's time to look at "THE CLOSE".

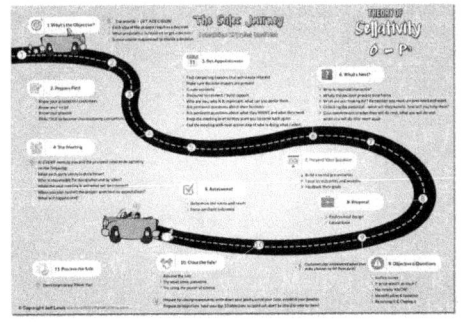

Get your beautiful FREE bonus
"Sales Journey Wall Chart"

Visit
www.sellativitysolutions.com

CHAPTER EIGHT

Closing the Sale

The key to closing the sale begins and ends with CONFIDENCE. Confidence in yourself, confidence in your abilities, and confidence in the product or service you are offering. With confidence you can enter into the final stages of securing the sale without hesitation and without fear of rejection. It seems today that the number-one reason for salespeople failing to close the sale is directly related to a fear of rejection.

The fear that the customer may say no. The funny thing is with this, of course, is that if you ask… they may say YES! Yet, many salespeople shy away from asking for the order because they are uncomfortable with the unknown. That place in time where the unknown result exists, where time stands still, that awkward gap when the air is heavy and no-one is speaking.

There also exists this uneasy feeling that maybe they (the salesperson) are taking advantage of the customer by making this sale. Now I want to pause right here and get something clearly identified… there is the professional sales environment, where a product or service is exchanged for payment. And there is the unprofessional realm of sales which is taking advantage of or conning the customer into paying more than is acceptable or completely "stealing" from the customer, and this is where con artists operate.

We all know what con artists are up to, don't we? These are smooth talkers and slick operators who take advantage of unsuspecting people in order to steal their money.

I say steal because this is what is taking place. If customers are paying more for a service or product than is acceptable or they are paying for something that essentially does not exist, then they have been conned by thieves posing as salespeople. Con artists as a profession are short lived simply because they can never stay in one place very long due to the fact that their non-delivery on their promises soon becomes noticeable and word gets around fast. Like any illegal activity involving criminal activity, sooner or later it catches up with you. The pressures of constantly operating on the edge takes it toll.

But let's talk about Professional selling and why it is that some salespeople have a complex or uneasiness about closing the sale. I will use an example shared with me early in my career. One day, after closing an especially big sale, I made a somewhat arrogant remark to my sales manager regarding the "big score" just made.

He reminded me of a particular principle that Zig Ziglar had used to establish the value of the sale to the CUSTOMER. He said (in paraphrase), when you make a sale and realise that you have just earned $100 (as an example amount of commission for the sale)… who has received the better end of the deal, you or the customer?

You as the salesperson will now envisage the ways you will spend your earnings or commission, and maybe you will buy something you have been wanting or pay bills, or save for a special purpose, etc. The point being, you will quickly spend the earnings you just made on the sale conducted. Yes, you have benefited, to be sure, and well you should. However, the customer is going to receive the benefits of the product you have sold him for how long?

Months… years…? Long after you spent your commission, the customer will be enjoying the benefits of what you have sold him, and therefore, the customer is the big winner. Long term benefits for the amount of money exchanged will satisfy the customer for years to come, and if the sale was handled professionally, the customer will recount his satisfaction with the product or service AND your professionalism to many other friends and associates.

That is what creates a successful and professional salesperson, one who is proud to be associated with his product and service and relies on the recommendations and referrals in the community. This is the "win-win" scenario that makes successful salespeople successful.

With that, I realised that this was not a contest to prove how good I was at sales. Arrogance and boasting about what a score I had made did little to encourage long term success.

What this attitude toward making sales did was set me up for stark realisation that customers would soon see the greed or desire to score in my presentations. Customers are not stupid, and they certainly pick up on body language, attitude, desire, confidence, arrogance, etc. Once you start down that path, it is very treacherous and difficult to recover from without help. And in this case, I was receiving help at a very appropriate time – immediately after I proclaimed my mastery of that recent sale.

Do not get me wrong, there is nothing wrong with celebrating a successful sale and feeling joy for doing a good job. You should reward yourself for doing a good job, and you should be excited for making big sales, but at the same time it should be tempered with the realisation that the customer ALSO made a good deal.

The customer ALSO won, he received the value of your product or service which is going to serve him well for years to come.

So back to my initial point – confidence and ridding yourself of that awkward feeling of taking advantage or 'scoring' the big sale. If you are selling a credible product or service at a credible price, then the customer is winning. He is winning because he is going to receive the benefits of this product or service for a long term or for the period required.

He is getting justifiable results and benefits for the price being paid. You have nothing to feel guilty about or to feel awkward about. You should be stating with confidence that the benefits of your product or service far exceed the price being paid and the customer will be receiving substantial results because of the decision they are making… therefore… how would they like to pay for it?

And that is confidence. Confidence in yourself, your worth (you are entitled to receive compensation or commission for your work, aren't you?), your professionalism, your product and your service. When you are able to see your value and the value of what you are selling, then asking for the order becomes a comfortable transition in the process, nothing more than the presentation itself, and certainly not worthy of hesitation.

In real terms, closing the sale is nothing more than confirming or finalising what has already taken place during your presentation. If you have followed your script, asked the right questions and received affirmative responses from your customer, then closing the sale is really just recording the details and receiving payment. Closing is a continuation of the process, the final step taken to reach the finish line.

Problems only arise when the salesperson is not confident in his process or presentation. This generally leads to their inability to ask for the order. Typically you will see salespeople begin to dance around the issue, trying to find a way to lead the customer to a conclusion, hoping that the customer will actually tell them to go ahead and write it up.

The view that I adhere to is the following: open with your best and close with your second best. The reason behind this is simple. Your initial three minutes is when you set the tone for your presentation. During this time, your preparedness is on display. You are confident, knowledgeable, personable, professional, communicative, friendly and ready… or you are lacking in some, all or a few of the traits required gaining the attention and respect of the customer.

Once again I recommend that you write out your script, beginning with your introduction and lead-in to your presentation. It is here that you make that critical first impression. It is here that you capture the interest of your customer. If you miss this opportunity you miss the golden moment that separates 'fair to good' salespeople from the elite professionals. It is here that separates the wheat from the chaff.

While it is possible to regain that momentum during your presentation, it is always an uphill battle and my view is, why make it harder on yourself? Closing, as well can bring back many sales which may have been damaged in the early moments and many salespeople think it is better to practice and concentrate on their closing, thus spending the majority of their time on this aspect of the process because they think this is where the results rest.

I agree that many sales can be salvaged by closing well; however, the following subconscious issues come into play:

Customers will be carrying a certain level of mistrust or unsurety about you because they were not impressed in the first few minutes. This could lead to buyer's remorse where customers make an initial sale with you but change their mind soon after you leave. Many customers then cancel their sale and their payment leaving you wondering why or what happened.

Customers will begin to ask for time to consider your offer as they may not be confident in you due to initial reservations regarding how the salesperson began their process. Customers feel uneasy as if they are being pressured because the closing may seem stronger than the presentation.

All in all, the most natural way to close is simply a continuation of the same professional process that you have followed throughout the introduction, presentation and finalisation of the sales offer.

I have supplied examples earlier in Chapters 2 and 3 of how to prepare the customer for making decisions. This should be part of the initial few minutes during your introduction. This is where and when you establish your professionalism. During this introduction period when you inform the customer what they may expect from you and in return what you will expect from them, this is when the customer recognizes that you are prepared and professional.

When you help them realize that you know what you are doing and that time is valuable to both the customer and yourself, this is when the customer gets comfortable with what you have to show them.

They know that this is not going to be a drawn out affair. They know it has a purpose and an end. They know you are here to conduct business and help them and, with this in mind, they become an ally in helping you finalise what you have started.

In the art of closing there are more than two-hundred types or patterns of "closes" that can be applied. Each one patterned or applicable to specific personalities or profiles shown by the customer during the sales process.

Zig Ziglar has a specific book designed and dedicated to "closes" and in there he identifies more than two-hundred and fifty complete with identities, traits to recognise, manner in which to apply specific closes, reasons to use specific closes and stories to assist with these "closes".

At one point in time when I was working as a self-sustaining salesperson I estimate I knew two-hundred specific "closes" by memory. That meaning, I had memorised more than two-hundred specific patterns of "closes" to be used according to how the customer represented themselves during my presentation.

Let me mention a part of my time spent working selling time share type vacation plans. Through my experiences of direct sales with door to door selling and then managing and teaching salespeople in this field, I had grown my closing percentage substantially and I was confident in my abilities to apply these principles to other areas of sales opportunities.

The opportunity to sell time share vacation plans was intriguing, exciting and challenging.

When I arrived on the scene at the offices, I learned that there was a very distinctive air about how the salespeople conducted their business. It was borderline arrogance and bravado. Bragging and beating of chest (like the King of the Apes style) was standard practice among those who were managers, team leaders and top salespeople at the respective branch offices (there were several branches of the same operation around the city).

Being the 'new' kid on the block, I was paired with the leading manager at the time who would show me the ropes and get me trained up in the art of selling the package on offer. What I quickly realised was that they too had discovered the success of using a scripted presentation of sorts. They all taught the process in the same sequence, and they followed a scripted closing sequence to a degree, but this is where the similarity ended. While they showed the process in the same general manner, there was nothing written to actually learn from.

It was all mentally scripted in the sense that each salesperson tended to mimic or clone from the one before them who had trained them. The result was a bit of 'broken telephone' if you have ever played that game? The game originates with one person being presented with a saying or scripted sentence or two. The lead person must memorise this script and then whisper their interpretation of this script into the next person's ear.

Each person in succession then repeats, to the best of their ability, what they remember from what was whispered to them. As the chain of people progresses, the message gets revised, shortened, amended and then finally relayed through the final person to the end result.

Needless to say, the more people involved in the chain, the more likely the fact that the end message is nowhere near to what was originally quoted. It makes for great fun and relevance when using this example for teaching the effectiveness of verbal communication. Everyone clearly sees what can happen when a message is relayed through a business while being reliant on each person saying exactly the same thing. It rarely, if ever, happens and the message gets corrupted through no fault of any one individual.

Well, the time share business I had entered was no different. While there was a resemblance of the same message being used by the various salespeople in the center, each person had taken it upon themselves to differentiate or decorate their version with their own perspective of the offer. When it came to the closing sequence, once again, there was a similar vein represented, but the finishing touches were left to each individual to embellish and create on their own.

Now there is a lot to be said for individual flair and professionalism and I certainly agree with salespeople inserting and building their own manner in which they present, but I also rely on the proven methods and continually remind salespeople to adhere to the guidelines while inserting their own individual-isms. What I found instead was each salesperson thinking and feeling their way was best and the results were such that there was an accepted ratio of what was considered and rewarded as good results.

There was an established percentage among the centers (branches) of 22% - 25% success in closing sales per salesperson. Overall, each branch was on a target requirement of 20% taking into account that not all salespeople would be hitting these targets consistently and some of the salespeople would be overachieving on these percentages. I recognised that this was considered acceptable results in the industry for direct sales in a time share type business such as this, yet I refused to believe this was acceptable for me. Having spent five years in direct door to door selling and training of salespeople, I refused to accept that I was going to spend the amount of time required to achieve such poor results. This position was part-time in the sense that I would work from 5 -10 p.m. only during the week and Saturday mornings until lunch time.

Since I had a "regular" job as the sales manager for an oil company during my "regular" work day, I was looking for a challenge and opportunity to keep my skills sharp and earn additional money while enjoying an evening opportunity with a cool atmosphere and fun environment.

My first order of business was to confirm in my own mind that what I was selling had benefit and value to the customer. Without this, it would be a con job and a product that I would not be able to sell, as I valued my professional relationship with the sales profession. As related above, once I am convinced that the customer is receiving value beyond the price being paid and the long terms results are synonymous with satisfaction, then I can immerse myself into writing a successful script.

Through investigating what was offered and available to the customer, I was convinced this was a very cool vacation package and one that I would buy myself. It generally provided customers with five years and seven weeks of vacations in often very exotic places. I began my script within one week of watching and learning.

What was evident and apparent to me in the business, was the fact that the salespeople were missing the first essential piece of the puzzle. Because customers had been phoned and invited to come see what the travel package was all about, the salespeople assumed that these customers already knew what they wanted or expected. The salespeople gave a cursory walk through the sites owned by the business and then moved into small offices to discuss how the program would work for them. No excitement, no investigation or enquiry into what the customer wanted, just a straight jump into the program and roll on through to closing.

Most of the time the closing consisted of complex payment plans with extended monthly and / or annual terms. The salespeople felt safe to offer these options because they were not confident in themselves and their abilities to ASK for the money, and they were not confident in the product because they felt a need to oversell on the product offering and undersell on how the customer could take advantage of it. This tended to confuse the customer and make the customer question whether the product or price was not suitable. What resulted were eight out of ten customers asking for time to consider the offering while making promises to call back, and salespeople ridiculously chasing customers for days trying to finalise these decisions.

Often without success of course – and in the few rare instances call back sales resulted, they were often accompanied with discounts and concessions in order to secure the deal. These concessions were most often direct reductions in salesperson's commissions in order to finalise. And the salespeople seemed happy to give away their earnings in exchange for a sale on the board and a "success" notch on their stats.

Salespeople were closely monitored and training was a big part of the job, which was encouraging, but the hard facts were that if salespeople did not maintain at least a 22% success ratio over the course of eight weeks, they were released. And sadly, there was a bit of revolving door activity in the business and management seemed to accept this. Their view was that new salespeople were excited and enthusiastic and sales resulted because of this, so the business view was, train, mentor and let them go. If they sell, great, if not... next!

When I negotiated my terms for joining the business, the management knew I came from a direct sales background and were very excited to get me on board. Once I understood what was involved in the sale, I requested preferential terms for me IF I was able to secure cash deals. Cash deals involved cash, check, and credit card.

The management was somewhat concerned with this decision, as the terms and facilities were a big part of their business and financing represented a significant percentage of their revenue. They did, however, recognize that cash flow and money in their account immediately was a huge incentive for them if it could be achieved, which until that time was not a big part of their success.

In order to achieve success for both sides (management and myself) I stated that I would achieve no less than 40% success rate per week and in exchange they would pay me a set amount per sale closed based on these terms. Initially they were reluctant and skeptical because they had not had anyone maintain a 40% closing ratio or better up until that time, but they were also curious to see if it could be done, so we agreed.

Even though I was able to show them that I had maintained a 60% closure rate in door-to-door book selling (based on presentations given… not every single door!), they thought this was being inflated and massaged somehow and could not believe this ratio to be true. So a challenge was set down, and accepted. I would be the test case, the guinea pig for this new initiative.

More than twenty years have past since I worked in this business, but the script I established is still fresh in my mind because I worked so hard to ensure its success. I am going to recount some of the process for you now to use as an example. What I found was that an initial attention grabber was required and then an exciting tour of the possibilities, a flight into the imagination of the customer to enthrall them and excite them, and then finally, a nice easy and simple way to pay for the enjoyment of the program.

A few points to understand… customers were telephoned and appointments were set for them to come in and view the offer and receive a gift holiday of some sort should they choose not to participate. Only so many prospective customers would be invited per evening as time allowed for only so many to be seen by the salespeople in the time allotted. Normally a salesperson if he followed his process properly could see two families or couples per evening. The salespeople worked in shifts with the most successful salespeople receiving the first incoming customers and then each subsequent salesperson would be linked with the next customer arrival.

As each salesperson would complete their time with the customer, either a sale would result or the non-successful customer would be ushered through to the "gift" department where a salesperson there would show them a discount flight package available to them for flights if they were interested, or they would receive their gift and head home. If a successful sale was made, the salesperson would move immediately to the top of the list and get the opportunity to receive the very next customer on the list. The thinking was that success breeds success and when a salesperson has just made a sale, he is "hot" and no time was better to strike than immediate.

If a salesperson was able to establish nightly success he would be first on the list for the next evening and secure himself more opportunities to sell and therefore increase his and the company's prospects for sales success. If you add up a week's worth of customer opportunities you will see that it might amount to ten to fourteen customer per week including Saturday mornings.

If you were not that successful, your options would be reduced to maybe eight to ten as you sat lower on the list. My plan was to see at least twelve per week and close eight of those or ten out of fifteen… I wanted 67%. I needed to be on the top of the list to do this and therefore needed sustained success, the script emerged:

My script began with an arrival, not just an entrance or introduction, which would not do. When the customers arrived they were seated in a lounge style reception area, sofa's, comfortable armchairs, TV's showing vacation sites, RCI time share locations, coffee and snacks were served and there were generally twelve to twenty people present (six to ten couples or families) and each of them somewhat apprehensive as to what was going to take place next.

Some of them talking together, trying to guess what would happen next, and it did not help if some salesperson stealthily swept around the corner, quietly asked who the "Smith's" were and then quietly introduced himself and asked them if they would follow him to his office. The setting lent itself to suspicion and nervous energy. I decided that I needed an arrival – a grand entrance to get their attention and create some positive energy, so I would leap around the corner, arms open wide and announce – "It's me – hurray!

Who wants to go on vacation?! Where are those lucky people, the Smith's?!" and then I would swoop over to them and say loud enough for everyone to hear – "if you could have the dream vacation, where would you like to go… have you ever thought about that?… well that's what I am here to help you achieve – that dream vacation, so where would you like to go? How about you start telling me, while we go take a tour of the possibilities, please follow me!"

This intro ensured I had their attention, lifted their enthusiasm levels, got them excited, got them thinking and created curiosity. They wanted to see what I was talking about, and so did everyone else in the place. Every salesperson benefited from my introduction and it took less than one week for me to be ensured of the first 'up' each evening. Not only did that create more opportunities for me with subsequent customers each evening, but it also set the tone for the evening, and no-one in front of me could sidetrack the path I wanted my customers to travel with me.

Next, I would walk them through six sites which were owned by the company in various locations (these were always preferable sites to encourage customers to utilise in their travel packages because we owned them and could better utilise and enable bookings), and as I did this, I would ask them if they ever considered going there, and could they imagine themselves being there on vacation. This would get their imagination working as they pictured all these sites that they may have never considered before. As I would conclude the tour (pictured sites on a central wall in the middle of the offices), I would say to them that even if they had never considered these locations before, maybe because of finances or planning or availability, that is what I was there for – to help this become a reality… and for a LOT less than they would have ever imagined. With that I would invite them into my office where I would show them how they could take advantage of this great opportunity.

Through all this I would like to point out that all of my conversations were thought out and scripted. Everything referred to 'would' instead of 'could' in the sense that I would relate to them, that this is how they 'would' take advantage of the location, this is where they would go, this is where they would stay, this is how they would get there, this is how they would be treated, this is how they would enjoy it… it was not a reference to this is where they 'could' stay, this is how they 'could' get there, this is how they 'could' enjoy themselves.

All these references were subtle, but they were all designed to plant seeds, to subconsciously connect them to seeing themselves there, all designed to have the Smith's place themselves in the scene. Words and use of those words are important – actually vitally important – and that is why I spend time listening to my script, reading and saying the lines over and over to ensure it sounds right, conveys the right message and connects the customer to the right realisation of them confirming the sale.

Once in my office, I would say, "Now that you can see yourselves enjoying your vacation at some of these fantastic locations, allow me to show you how you can take advantage of this incredible program.

Because we help so many families such as yours take advantage of fabulous vacations like these, we are able to negotiate tremendous package deals which mean that you get to enjoy seven fantastic vacation packages over a five year period at unbelievable prices…"
I would then pause and insert the most important ingredient of my script – the removal of the "I want to think about it" objection. At this point, the customer is excited, interested, curious, anxious and captivated by everything that has taken place to this point, and now I need to insert the reality of why we were there together – the business aspect of the meeting.

"Mr & Mrs Smith, one thing I have learned from this business is the importance of making solid, clear and informed decisions. I have had the privilege of meeting and assisting numbers of families like yourselves, and the most important part of these opportunities is the understanding of the fact that the most relevant and logical time to make decisions is when the information is fresh and clear and answers to your questions are readily available right in front of you.

In all my years of sales, one fact stands clear, and that is that information presented is very quickly forgotten within twenty-four hours. Because our minds process so many bits of information, facts and information shown through a presentation or tour can quickly be lost, studies have shown that 80-90% of information presented will be forgotten or misinterpreted within twenty-four hours of subjects being removed from the facts.

Because of these reasons and because I get asked to see so many people, I am going to ask you one favor to help both of us, if you don't mind… and that is… when I am finished and have presented all the facts and information about the program, and while we are together and I have the opportunity to answer whatever questions you may have… and you can ask whatever you like, don't be shy or afraid to ask, there are no wrong or silly questions (smile on face)… that when we arrive at the final destination together, that you either say yes, you would like to take advantage of the program, or no, you wouldn't,… and that's fair isn't it?" No pressure, just information and assistance, o.k.?! (And I nod my head while looking directly at them. I want assurance now from them that they agree) and I await their reply. More than 90% of the time it is a "yes, that is fair and acceptable".

On the occasions where they question this, I take just a few moments to reassure them I only want what is best for them and the best setting for them to make a decision. I once again assure them that due to the number of people I see and the demand for the program, I will not be able to follow up nor extend the offer after we finish tonight. I once again assure them that this is not a pressurised environment and should they feel that this is not suited to them, that is fine with me and we will remain friends and they will receive their gift as promised with no hassles.

I only want them to be able to make a clear decision and will assist them to do that… and I appeal to their abilities as mums, dads or business people to understand the need for decisions in an everyday situational society and once more ask for their assistance in doing me this favour. At this point, the acceptance rate is approximately 98-99%. In those very rare cases where they do not feel they can do that, I ask why, attempt to calm their fears and if they simply do not agree with being favorable to making decisions, I ask them if I could refer them to another salesperson who may have capabilities to follow up, or if they would like to accept our thanks and the gift and we will excuse them from the presentation. I am always kind and respectful and do not just dismiss customers unjustifiably. However, on the very, very rare occasion where customers have chosen not to make decisions, I find it best to encourage them to seek other assistance as my time is limited and I would not like to enter into promises or obligations to follow up when I know I cannot fulfill this obligation.

Remember, the main emphasis here is to ensure the customer knows you mean business. You are not there to be a professional visitor. Some salespeople think they are there to humor customers and entertain them for an hour and then say thanks, that was fun. Professional visitors may be suitable in a service industry where customer retention and satisfaction is required. Professional visitors then go and visit clients and listen to what they have to say, and hopefully return with usable information to ensure customer retention and satisfaction. But salespeople are NOT professional visitors – they need to make sales, they need to get decisions (and hopefully favorable ones!), but they are not there to entertain and then wave goodbye without ever asking for the business.

Once the "I want to think about it / decision making" agreement is taken care of, I proceed to outline how the program will work and how they will take advantage of it. You will notice again, I say 'would' and 'will' as opposed to 'could' and 'can'. Test it yourself, you will see what the difference is. As I reach the final bend heading into the "close" I lead in with:

"Mr. & Mrs. X, now that we have established the fact that you like to go on vacation (big smile!), the only remaining question would be how many vacations would you like to take in the next five years… As you are now aware, there is a plan or program designed to fit your plans and budget. Of the plans I have shown you, plan A which is the "Deluxe" plan and provides you with XXX over the course of the five years and the price is $XXX, or plan B which is the "Special" plan and provides you with XXX, and the price is $XXX, or plan C which is the "Starter" plan and provides you with XXX, for the price of $XXX. So Mr. and Mrs. X, of the Deluxe plan, the Special plan or the Starter plan, which of the vacation plans would be best for you?" And I stay silent; I am now waiting on them to choose what they like best.

When they do, and they will, or they will ask a few questions about the plans again – and this is fine, this is just re-affirming their inclination, (let's say they choose plan B) – I would then say "fine, great choice, you are going to love your vacations… and there are a few ways you can take care of that. We offer cash… cash always works of course (big smile), check, or credit card where you may have your own terms already in place with your bank or credit card facility - Of the methods available to you, which would work best for you, cash check or credit card?" and I stay silent.

Because I had earlier explained the pricing with each option and asserted the benefits with the options at that time, it means that during the close, it is simply choices being made as opposed to 'yes or no' type decisions. I will explain in more detail in the next chapter regarding types of closes and simple methods to begin with that are most effective. I have just showcased an example of the prime closing sequence that I have utilised for years, and the one that I find most effective in almost all cases.

What I am trying to highlight here is that once you follow your script and process you can easily flow into the close and effectively finalise the customers confirmation of the sale complete with choice and method of payment.

What is most interesting with this method I employed is the fact that choices are limited to no more than three choices per category; such as, choices of plans on offer – three. Choices of payment options – just three… cash, check or credit card. This limits the amount of searching or choosing the customer is required to perform. Always make it simple and easy – no more than three choice options.

Otherwise, confusion sets in. Think of the times that too many options exist, all you want to do is run away and have time to consider all the options. Too many options available is asking for trouble. When the salesperson says you can have this, or this, or this, or this or this… and you can pay for it like this, or this, or this, or this, it creates a logjam in your head and you want time to sort it all out. In a sales situation where customer clarity is important and they need to understand what you are asking them to decide on, take time to reduce your options and choices to what is best suited to the customer.

Even if you have many options, this is where professional selling is an art; it is up to you the salesperson to listen to the requests and requirements, narrow down the choice options and offerings to a limited few and then present them in the most attractive manner while explaining to the customer that you have proposed three solutions that you, as the professional consultant, feel are best suited to the customer, and which one do they feel is best for them!

Offering choices (and no more than three) makes it a whole lot easier for the customer to choose A, B or C as opposed to first deciding yes or no they want a solution from you and then having to make choices of which one after they first have to choose yes or no to go with you. Remove the 'yes or no' from the equation. When I would continue into my close on the travel packages, it was always which one… as opposed to yes or no, would you like it.

To finish my story, and I trust it was informative as well as enjoyable, within three weeks my closing percentage was 60% and over the course of the reminder of my time there became 67%. I was able to regularly close eight of twelve, ten of fifteen, etc. and I would assume (there is a hint there for the next chapter), that doubts in my method – my "Theory of Sellativity" – were put to rest. I think that the company was happy and continued to utilise the "Theory" after I moved on.

Opportunities to travel internationally and work internationally arose about a year later and new global challenges waited, so my time in direct sales seemed to be coming to a close in the USA. Exciting new projects and cultures were calling me now and testing my "Theory" on the world stage was an exciting prospect. The final chapter of my book will relate a brief historical account of my sales journey to date, but for now, let's get on with closing the sale!

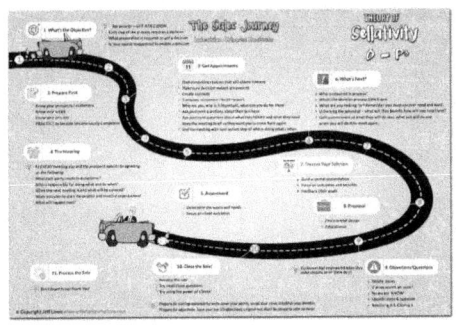

Get your beautiful FREE bonus
"Sales Journey Wall Chart"

Visit
www.sellativitysolutions.com

CHAPTER NINE

Closing Technique

As stated in Chapter 8, there are more than two-hundred distinct closing techniques or designed closes according to situational settings. As you progress and grow you will develop your own repertoire of closes based on your unique or specific selling arena. Many situations will arise that will call on your skill and knowledge to match the situation with the perfect close, and this will be exciting and motivating to your career. But for now I am going to stick to the basics. The tried and tested – the battle tested – method that proves itself worthy of the challenge every single time.

Earlier in the book we talked about surgeons, lawyers, accountants and specialists who relied on tried and true procedures. Once again call to your imagination a surgeon performing a sensitive procedure. He doesn't change the procedure each time he performs such a sensitive procedure, he follows the same process and same procedure every time, knowing that following the procedure elicits the very best chance for success.

Tried and true methods are just that – tried and tested to be true. Theories investigated and under scrutiny are tried and tested to establish the truth, the outcome and the result. Think of the inventors down through history who tried time after time to establish a result, an invention, a cure. It often took hundreds of attempts, hundreds of methods and procedures were tried, tested and reworked until success was achieved. The light bulb, electricity, the telephone, communication, engines, cars, flight, airplanes, jets, space travel; all come with tried and tested theories, methods, procedures and process mechanisms that are proven. And with these proven successes, methods and procedures are established and published so that all may benefit from the enormous amount of work that went into these breakthroughs.

Thus, after twenty-five years of experimenting, testing, tuning and trying various "closes", I am pleased to unveil my easy and simple close for all occasions…

It is **'The ASSUMPTIVE ACTION CHOICE'** close.

Let me break this down for you so that you are able to understand each facet of the close and how it all works together in order to Get the Decision. When you grasp the power behind this closing sequence, in conjunction with your sales process, you will recognise just how easy it is to achieve the goal of Getting A Decision every time and all-the-time.

Let's do a quick review – Up to this point we established how necessary it is to be prepared, to have scripted your sales process, to have practiced until you know your presentation and process adequately. I say adequately because you will also recall that like with any new career, new adventure, new undertaking or new opportunity there comes with these the four steps to professionalism. Remember these:

1. Unconsciously incompetent – you don't know that you do not know. Intricacies or details of the new opportunity don't even exist for you because you don't even know they exist. Until something arises to draw your attention to the opportunity and the requirements contained within, you are oblivious to what is required or what is required of you.
2. Consciously incompetent – now you know that you do not know. Study is required, understanding of the opportunity, investigation, questions arise and facts are discovered that allow you to understand that you now know that this project or opportunity has more involved in it than

you may have realised… or at least are realising now.

3. Consciously competent – through study, practice, investigation, trial & error, testing, questioning, and essentially kicking the tires of the situation / opportunity you become competent to do the job. Maybe it is an apprenticeship, or junior position, but you now begin working in the opportunity, showing competence through following the procedures and process that you have studied, internalised and practiced.

4. Unconsciously Competent – a seasoned veteran, an expert, a specialist, a professional. Experience, trials and tribulation have tested you and you have become competent in the position, able to perform at an extremely high performance capability without having to think twice about it. Your training and experience has led you to that professional level associated with experts. You are now able to perform under the most difficult circumstances as a matter of precision and efficiency due to your expertise.

Therefore, "The Assumptive Action Choice" close compliments the stages listed above. You didn't or don't know what it is, you now know it exists and want to know, and only through absorbing the process of this close inside your sales process will you realise the success you strive for. Closing like the other aspects of the sales process involves learning the process, writing the script, testing and practicing and then implementing and using it. As in step #3, you will need to test your closing process along with your sales process in real, live environments.

As long as you are following the method and the theory, you will find you becoming consciously competent. You will need to think and reflect a bit on where you are and what you need to do, but I will provide some examples to learn from and with this you can build your foundation and practice to gain that consciously competent reality you seek.

Closing on its own is not the answer. The introduction where you gain attention, trust and believability is the foundation for your later success when the closing sequence is managed well. The body of your presentation is just as important because it is here that you are establishing what the choices are and what the prices are that accompany those choices.

It is also here that you establish what the customer likes, what they need to satisfy their wants and what your product or service does to benefit them in their desire to satisfy those requirements. Once you perform the sales process accordingly you will find that the close I am outlining for you in this chapter to be the icing on the cake. It will be like the Grand Finale to a brilliant fireworks show.

'The ASSUMPTIVE ACTION CHOICE' close begins with the assumption that the customer is buying, and that is the intention isn't it... you are not a professional visitor, are you? All of the customer buying signs throughout your introduction – your informative interlude where you gain acceptance of the decision making requirement, your presentation where you outline features and benefits – finally brings you to the final stages of confirming the sale where the customer will now choose which options and payment terms will best suit their requirements.

The assumption process is the natural result because you have done all the right things and asked all the right questions and the customer has been in agreement with you throughout the process.

It is now simply a matter of deciding what the customer will purchase – NOT IF they will purchase. The Assumptive role in the close is the understanding that they ARE buying, it is only left to you to ask them which options they prefer. Assumption closes assume you and the customer are on the same page, and this is up to you to control. All you have to do is be confident, move forward and take the second phase of the close – ACTION.

The Action of the close is related to the action you take as you enter into the closing sequence. You take Action by picking up the agreement, filling in customer details, establishing terms, dates, and definitive action points while you offer the CHOICES.

Action is identified in what you do. You take action. You do not sit passively and wait for the client to exclaim that he wants it, and what does he have to do to get it. Remember, you are taking assumptive action – that means the customer is buying, and you are taking action by offering the choices and final options – this leads directly into the CHOICE phase of the Assumptive Action.

The Choice activity of the closing sequence becomes the choices you now offer. The Choice segment incorporates all aspects of the close because you are assuming they are buying… unless they stop you. This is key, because you must be moving through your actions and choices with great confidence; after all, you are offering a great product or service at a great price, what is not to like!? At the choice offerings, the choices must be clear, concise and involve no more than three choices per option.

Each option must get a choice response from the customer. Action – next choice offering, keep writing, get their choice, move onto payment options or terms, this is the final option or final choice and with this you are finalising and confirming the sale. You have asked what they want, how they want it, when they want it and how they are paying for it.

Remember from the previous chapter I say no more than three options to choose from per category or per offering because three options has been proven as the ultimate and maximum number of option that a customer can process intelligently and coherently without getting confused and requiring more time to consider the options. Think about your own buying trends.

When you are presented with numerous options and choices, it becomes overwhelming and confusing. Too many choices brings your brain to a standstill. It is like an overload and your mind says, hold on, this is too much input to assess and analyse, we are going to require more time to go through all this data. And what happens next... you ask for time to consider the choices. You ask for brochures and information on the choices while you go away to either consider the purchase, or surmise that the choices, options, pricing, or even the item itself is worth really buying anyway.

Too many options create a buying deadlock and can lose a sale completely. It also becomes too much for the salesperson to rattle off more than three choice options. When you offer a choice of A, B or C it is easy to quickly recount the benefits of each choice and allow the customer to choose what is best for them. You can even use your professionalism to suggest what you believe is the most beneficial choice for them based on what they have detailed for you throughout the sales process.

Generally you will have an insight into what the customer is leaning toward or what may best suit them, and with your choice options you may interject that option A may be the best suited for them based on what they are looking for, nevertheless you want them to know that option B or C also exists if they feel that may fit their requirement.

But when you start extending beyond three options, it becomes too much to relay while highlighting the benefits, and it becomes too much for the customer to remember, and therefore they stop listening and move directly into "I will need to think about this and consider all the options" mode.

Choice offerings are a key component to the process, so please understand that not offering choices will result in your sales process being reduced to a choice of either yes or no that the customer wants the product, because that is the only option being offered. That is not a strong position to be in because it leaves you with few alternatives.

If you state to the customer that this is the option you have worked out for them, what else are you going to ask them other than do they accept that or not? At this point you are backed into a corner, and most sales people paint themselves into this corner. You are now reliant on the customer to close the deal for you. This is where most sales people conduct business, and this is why 20% sales closure success is deemed acceptable. It is where the old axiom resides that everybody operates this way, so it must be the accepted method.

Two choice options are ideal because it is very easy to offer either this or that, which would you prefer.

If your product or service allows for the ability to offer choice options as either this or that, it is an ideal position to be in because it is clear and easy for a customer to choose one or the other. It may also suit you best if you are new and just beginning or you are establishing your consciously competent position. The two choice option is easy to control and manage and easiest to remember.

The three choice option is the maximum, as I have stated, and I use this option in the majority of my sales opportunities because I find I can sense which option is most viable for the customer and offering three choices shows that we have varied and flexible offerings designed for them and nothing is being hidden from them. It is not as if a choice or possibility has been kept from them. For me, this further encourages the customer to trust and rely on my expertise because they can see I am hiding nothing from them and choices are offered to give them the best solution possible.

Finally – ACTION – hand them the order form, the agreement, the contract and ask for their o.k. – that's it… and be silent! You have done your work… like a surgeon, you have professionally proceeded through your opportunity with clinical expertise, and now like a surgeon tying the final suture closed to close the procedure – tie your lips closed and be quiet. It is now time for the customer to finalise his part of the journey… sign the sales order. Now is NOT the time to make any final offers or interject any more words of wisdom – just be quiet and let the body of you professional work speak for itself. I am emphasising this area of the close because the majority of sales opportunities are wasted here and lost here because the sales person gets uncomfortable and feels he has to say something. Or he feels compelled to add one little additional benefit or one little customer recommendation.

Maybe just a word of encouragement about what a great deal they are getting, or maybe just a little question to the customer as to whether he has any questions... arrrgh. This is when sales are lost. Not in the presentation, not in the close itself, but in those precious few moments when the sales person needs to be quiet and let the customer finalise his decision in his own head!

The customer just needs a few minutes to process his own thoughts. To validate his decision to purchase. To trace the steps of the process to ensure all his questions were answered, to ensure himself that this is what he wants, what he needs. To prove to himself the price is fair and just and the benefits compliment his willingness to pay the price. All these things race through the customer's mind when you are handing him the order forms to sign and IF you disturb him you disrupt the entire sales process you have just so painstakingly finished only moments before. Do yourself a very big favor here and practice keeping your mouth shut for three minutes. Just like you practice your presentation, practice sitting there quietly while the client reads through the order / agreement. THREE minutes – just be quiet. If you will do this, your sales success percentage will increase a minimum of 10% - just try it... test me and see if I am right.

A couple examples may help you prepare your closing script based on the Assumptive Action Choice close:

When I was selling books door to door (direct one call sales opportunities) this is the final segment to my sales process. Obviously the close was a continuation of the sales process I had scripted. As I would conclude my presentation highlighting the final product offers, I would simply transition into my close as follows...

CLOSE NUMBER ONE

"Mr. X, now that we have explored the options available I'm sure you'd agree with me that the life lessons contained in these stories will be a valuable asset to your family as your children rely on you to help them make good decisions growing up. In today's world, the more you can do to prepare your children for the choices they are being forced to make everyday, the more you can rest assured that the money invested in their education and character will make this set invaluable in your home.

I have highlighted the benefits of the different sets we offer to families such as yours and what I will do now is show you how we make them available to you as set offerings.

The first option is the "Deluxe" offering. In this set, what you will receive is the complete range which contains the children's set of XXXX, this of course provides you with the range of character building stories, practical educational volumes, informational and historical volumes, all designed to build character, assist with making good decisions, practical information to assist in their learning experience and, of course, the benefit of knowing the children have everything at their fingertips to help them… and this is peace of mind for you.

You know you are not left short-handed wondering if there was something you might try to find at a library or book store or something more you may have been able to do for them but didn't know where to find the right story or information. We then also compliment this with the volumes for mum and dad and for the kids as they grow up.

A complete historical set in more detail for you to enjoy, and finally the medical volumes which cover the widest range of medical related information outside of medical school (smile). This set is designed to help every family recognize and identify whatever illness or emergency that may occur, along with practical action to take to treat those emergencies or issues. The benefits of this of course are many including, emergency measures, preventative measures, education related to good health, and practical guidelines of what to do in case you are called upon to take action.

This "Deluxe" set is available for $XXX... or $XXX monthly on our easy terms plan.

Next, we have the "Special" set offering. In this "special" set, you will receive the children's range and a choice of either the historical set or the medical volumes. We find this is our most popular offering because families are so interested in the materials designed to help them especially with their children.

This "Special" set is available for $XXX ... or $XXX monthly on our easy terms plan.

Finally we have the "Beginner" set in which you will receive the children's practical story set only and a choice of one of the volumes designed for mum and dad – it is either the one historical volume X or the one medical volume X, either of these are designed to give practical use for you as parents.

The "Beginner" set is popular because it allows families to get started and introduce the value of reading and learning in the home, while providing for the ability to add on at a later date when you see the benefits of what the materials can do for your home.

Theory of Sellativity — Closing Technique

This "Beginner" set is available for $XXX… or $XXX monthly on our easy terms plan.

Obviously the biggest and best savings is available within the Deluxe and Special offerings. If you are like most families and like taking advantage of the best value for the money, I would recommend either of those offers… it really is up to you though, simply choose what you feel is the best option for your family. Mr. & Mrs. X, of the choices offered which do you prefer, Deluxe, Special or Beginner?" (And be quiet, they will think, discuss, answer… or ask your assistance to help them choose the best for their family. Do not say anything until they answer or ask for your help).

The customers chooses "special" – and I would then say, "and of the terms available… cash, cash always works (big smile), check, credit card or our easy terms plan… which plan would work best for you?" (And be quiet… again they will decide, discuss, answer or ask your opinion or assistance).

Because I had become a trusted consultant during my time with them, the customer will often ask for my assistance to help them decide. They will recognise that I am the expert and have the experience with hundreds of families so they will ask me to recommend to them what to do. When you are in this position, it's a position of trust and confidence and you must ensure you act in the best interest of the family as this will ensure long term success and future references to other families such as the customers themselves. Do not oversell just to get the sale because the customer is relying on you. It will not be long until they recognise you took advantage of them!

Theory of Sellativity — Closing Technique

While I am asking the customer for their choices, one of my action steps is to pick up the order form, start completing the customer information… name, address, etc. As they make their choices, I start recording those choices in the product selection section of the invoice… as I finish with asking which payment plan will work best for them, I simply make that final calculation and entry on the form and then take the final action…

"Mr. & Mrs. X, you have made a fantastic investment for you and your family and you will receive years of enjoyment and benefits, I commend you on your excellent choice. This is how it will work for you" – and here is when I turn the order form around and with my pen, I direct them through the order form, showing them what they are getting, and the price. I then refer to the total showing shipping and delivery, telling them when they will be receiving their set, and the final tally where I either explain to them how the payments will work or what the total is for them to pay. At that point, I simply ask them to O.K. the order so I can leave them their copy and send through the paperwork for the order to be shipped. With this, I place the order pad in their hands and release the pen from my hand for them to use while signing.

It is as simple and easy as that. A few subconscious things take place in my close that I would like to highlight for you…

1. In my closing, I always refer to "what they will receive" – it is a subconscious transfer of ownership, each time I relate what the option is on offer, I state that this is what they will receive.

2.   In my closing, I use terms such as "which will work best for you", "which do you prefer", "what would suit you best", "which choice do you like best". These phrases are tried and tested. Many years of working on the right scripting has resulted in these closing phrases. When using these phrases, they are comfortable and soft to the customer. They are not abrupt or direct in the sense that you are calling for a major decision and they must choose yes or no. They are simply making choices of preference. They are saying they prefer this to that, or this will work best, or this is what they prefer. Run it through your own thinking process. If at each of these junctures, I asked them if it met their needs or their requirements… or if they liked this or that… they could say no, or they could hesitate to assess whether it met their needs or requirements, this puts the closing sequence in jeopardy and hesitation can lead to no decision. Careful selection and use of words is always the key to the script. Ensure you take the time to reflect on what, how and why you are using the script that you are.

3.   In my closing, I am always taking action, progressing from one step to the next. There is no hesitation, and I am busy completing the order form while they are discussing their choices. Two things happen, One – they recognise that I am busy writing up their order, they know I am conducting business. Again, imagine that while I am asking them the questions I am simply sitting there, and the order form is sitting somewhere else… their view is they are simply answering preference questions… when I pick up the order form after this, it is like a big fright to them, they think "oh what is happening now, I thought we were just making choices", and the order form becomes a mental stumbling block if it has not been in use and visible.

Two – by continually writing and recording the details, when I arrive at the payment and signature point, everything is complete and ready to go. Again, without hesitation I am able to show them exactly what they are getting, for what price and how they will be paying for it. This allows me to transition through the final signature with no delay; no flashing red lights that the customer is now being asked to sign something...

4.   In my closing, I assume they are buying and ask for their O.K., as opposed to their signature – signature is a strange and forbidding term, it causes customers to visualise warning signals, red lights and cautionary roadblocks. When I ask for their O.K. so that I can leave them their copies and process the order, it is relaxed and comfortable and I am simply asking for their O.K. When salespeople start asking for a signature, it conjures up legal documentation and customers now want to refer to their legal department, financial department, etc. Always ensure you explain the terms and what they are signing... I always do, but I make it easy and simple and relaxed so that asking for their O.K. is relaxed and accepted, the customers see it as part of the process.

5.   In my closing, I am in control. I am directing the ship, steering and leading the customer in order to help them make solid, good choices. I do not throw the entire series of choices and payment options onto the table and ask the customer to tell me what he would like to do next! In my years of selling and training in sales, I am continuously frustrated and perplexed at how many salespeople go through such effort to present and get themselves into position to close the sale and then throw the whole thing on the table and ask the customer to tell them, the salesperson, what they would like to do next. Think how many times you have seen salespeople get to the final stage of closing the deal and then turn to the customer

and say, o.k. well, I have shown you everything, what would you like me to do next? It happens all the time, in some variation of the above scenario. The salesperson gets to the final step and leaves it to the customer to now close the sale.

6.   In my closing, I am in control and once the choice offerings are asked, I shut up. I will only respond once they have made the choice or asked for my help, which I will give through a recommendation in order to help them decide, and then I ask again which they prefer… and shut up. I require a response so I can move to the next step. If I don't get the response, how can I move on? Skip the step and continue to where? Think of that in a surgical operation, well we will just skip this step and move to the next?

7.   In my closing, I always make use of 'Good, Better, Best'. These options are progressive and allow you to build one upon the other. Huh? What if I said to you there might be a better option? Perhaps the customer has a 'good' product, service or solution they make use of… a viable option to offer is the possibility of something that may be 'better'. This way it does not detract from what they have, it just increases their desire to have 'better'. And if it is better, then perhaps there is a 'best' offer or solution for them. I always refer to what choice 'best' suits them or 'best' delivers what they want. Customers love to feel they are getting the 'best' and this is what you as a salesperson should be striving for (I also use this method in overcoming or handling objections – see Chapter 10).

My closing sequence presented as Option #1 was scripted more than twenty-three years ago, and while the Internet and computers today has replaced a lot of direct book selling, books still sell, and the closing sequence is easily adapted to include references to computers, Internet searches, etc. The materials could still be sold based on the fact that the books would be sitting right there, easy to use, easy to find, no prolonged searches and downloads, etc., so always keep in mind that this closing script was written years ago, yet is a framework and template that continues to be usable today.

I am going to offer my closing sequence for selling the travel plans, and then finally my closing sequence for the I.T. industry whether hardware or software consulting… it is all the same to me!!

CLOSE NUMBER TWO

While finishing my presentation of travel plan options; I lead into my close with the following:

"Mr. & Mrs. X, now that we have established the fact that you like to go on vacation (big smile!), the only remaining question would be how many vacations would you like to take in the next five years… As you are now aware, there is a plan or program designed to fit your plans and budget. Of the plans I have shown you, plan A which is the "Deluxe" plan and provides you with XXX over the course of the five years and the price is $XXX, or plan B which is the "Special" plan and provides you with XXX, and the price is $XXX, or plan C which is the "Starter" plan and provides you with XXX, for the price of $XXX. So Mr. and Mrs. X, of the Deluxe plan, the Special plan or the Starter plan, which of the vacation plans would be best for you?"

And I stay silent; I am now waiting on them to choose what they like best. When they do, and they will, or they will ask a few questions about the plans again – and this is fine, this is just re-affirming their inclination, (let's say they choose plan B) – I would then say "fine, great choice, you are going to love your vacations... and there are a few ways you can take care of that. We offer cash... cash always works of course (big smile), check, or credit card where you may have your own terms already in place with your bank or credit card facility – Of the methods available to you, which would work best for you, cash check or credit card?" and I stay silent.

You will notice that Option #2 is quite simple and straightforward. The customer likes to go on vacation, how many vacations they want to take are determined in the plans available and which plan suits the customer best. Which does the customer like and which payment option and the close is basically finished. Keep this always in mind; customers are not unable to make buying decisions or choices on how to pay. They do it all the time, check out their homes, cars, TV's, appliances, holidays, furniture etc. they buy things all the time and pay for it.

So why do we as salespeople need to be so cautious or timid to ask them to pay? If you ask, you may get... if you don't ask, you don't get!

This closing script is approximately twenty years old and once again taken from memory. Once you think, spend time, write and script your process, it is embedded in your head for life. The template and foundation are established and available for anytime you want to call on the knowledge, so write it down – don't just rely on me writing it in my book. I would safely assert that this closing script would still work today, the same principles still apply.

CLOSE NUMBER THREE

This one is the latest, written for the I.T. industry of which I have been a part now for fifteen years, in both hardware and software. Although the margins are tremendously different, the same rules and concerns apply in regards to customer requests and requirements.

"Mr. X, we have now been through a number of meetings with you, your financial people, your I.T. staff, etc. to determine the 'best' solutions for your company. We have assessed your requirements and your wants in an effort to deliver the 'best' fit according to your business and our solution. With that in mind, the only thing left to do is allow you to choose the solution you feel is best suited according to where your business is positioned in the market. We have prepared two solutions for you, the first one is an all encompassing solution that provides for all your wants and needs and will position you for internal and external growth for the next several years. This solution is capable of fulfilling all the current requirements and your upcoming future expectations. We have built into this solution room for growth and functionality to supply you with everything you have asked for in our meetings. The solution provides you with XXX and the price is $XXX.

The second solution is designed for your current requirements and meets the needs that you have outlined to us during our meetings. It also provides functionality and room for growth on a limited scale so that you get full use from the system and reap the benefits immediately once the installation and training is complete. This solution provides you with XXX and the price is $XXX.

Mr. X, the choice you have is do you take advantage of the all encompassing solution and pricing that accompanies this full solution so that you can amortise the cost across a number of years and provide for the price just this one time while enjoying the benefits of the full system over the next few years… or would you prefer to take advantage of the second solution which addresses all your current needs and functionality requirements while allowing for some growth in the near future. With the second solution, you are always able to upgrade and further enhance your system as and when you require it.

Mr X, which of the two solutions is best suited for you, which do you prefer?" (And be quiet!)

"Mr. X, that is a fine choice and will accomplish your goal of facilitating your business with the best solution possible in the least amount of time. As we have previously discussed, the payment terms will incorporate a 50% deposit against the product requirement, and the implementation and installation as well as the training will be invoiced according to our terms for you at the time of completion per site. The terms are shown for you here in our agreement and as each site is complete we will both have documentation related to the daily task sheets signed off and will then invoice accordingly for this segment of our work with you (Through this process I am showing the customer the terms for consulting, implementation, estimated time requirements per site and training costs).

My last bit of housekeeping to ensure we are both on the same page is to ask you when you would like us to begin so we can arrange schedules and personnel.

Mr X, what time frame do you have in mind, would you like us to start immediately or two weeks from now… here is a calendar, what dates suit you best? (And be quiet)

Mr X, I just need your O.K. here to get things started…" (show signature line on the agreement and hand him the pen).

The main requirement of the salesperson in a multiple meeting, or longer sales cycle process is to continually update the customer on the process and what you are doing next. The next meeting, the next requirement, the next deadline, etc. while you meet with admin departments, financial departments, I.T. departments to assess requirements, ensure you are building your solution accordingly.

Your presentation phase should address the needs and wants of the customer, and allow you to build your final proposal documentation to attend the final meeting with the decision makers.

If you have done this, then the final meeting is a sales confirmation meeting and the assisting of the customer to make the best choice for his business. In these finalisation meetings, it is necessary to offer as few choices as possible so as to not confuse the process and prompt the decision makers to delay a decision.

If necessary, encourage them to discuss the final two options together while you step out of the room and allow them to get to a decision. Help them by recommending what you believe to be the best solution for them.

I have now been involved with numerous multi-national group companies that operate in many countries and cultures that are diverse and require easy to use yet sophisticated systems and my success rate for closing these large deals is higher than 60% (if I told you the actual percentage you would think I am making it up).

The reason my closing sequence works is because I have prepared the decision makers to make a decision – remember my earlier request to ensure they will make a decision – and I have prepared solutions suited to them based on their requirements instead of my own… and I limit the choices to two (2).

This or that, which one is best for you. In regards to corporate decisions, it is the responsibility of the salesperson to control the flow and assist with the final decision making. In these situations, either choice is a "win" so be sure to work with them to ensure they are able to see this and are willing to make a decision. There is no right or wrong when you have presented workable solutions for the customer, simply which one becomes the "best" decision.

In conclusion to the closing chapters, many closes could be presented, but I have chosen to reflect for you the ONE that is most effective, time tested, tried and true and has a success rate of 60% or better if you script it out and incorporate it into your process. If you want further insight into the world of closing – get Zig Ziglar's 'The secrets of closing the sale'.

Finally on this section I will say this. While you are learning and growing and experimenting and trying, keep this in mind – whatever happens, whether the presentation has gone well or poorly, ask for the order! Yes, ask for the order.

Actual sales evidence has proven that if you just ask for the order, your sales success will increase at least 10%. So even if you get stuck or lost or thrown off your course, ask the customer if you could please have their order. 'May I please have your order' is a sure fire way to ask for a decision! Many sales have been rescued or salvaged simply by asking for the order. Customers often want what you are selling, and only the salesperson is getting in the way of the sale. When that happens just ask, and you may get. If you don't ask, you don't get. If you need proof, go try it!

Next up, what do you do when the customer objects or seems to be firmly saying no?

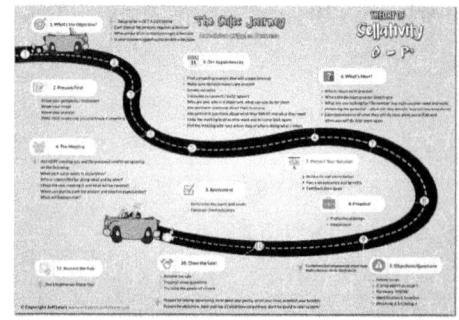

Get your beautiful FREE bonus
"Sales Journey Wall Chart"

Visit
www.sellativitysolutions.com

CHAPTER TEN

Overcoming Objections

Objections are as much a part of the sales process as the presentation itself. Seldom does it occur that a sale is closed without at least one objection or query. Objections should be viewed as just that, queries. What customers are saying when they say 'no' is more accurately, 'know', as in they do not 'know' enough yet to make a final buying decision. Customers will make decisions when they have enough solid information to make clear choices and when they are comfortable with the offer. Otherwise, they will ask questions, make further enquiries or call upon objections in order to slow the process down and ensure that they are getting all the information they require.

I have learned over the years that objections are my friends because they help uncover the true questions that lie beneath the surface. Without objections the salesperson can end their sales call without knowing what the real reason is behind the customers' indecision or non-buying reluctance. Conjecture creeps in and salespeople start to rationalise why the customer did not buy.

Salespeople rationalise their own failure through placing blame or fault on any number of excuses that may have arisen from the customer, or lack of closing (getting a decision) on the part of the salesperson. When you realise that customers are saying 'know', as in I need to know more information before I can decide, then you are able to ask the right questions in return to ensure the customer understands what the offer entails.

Customers will make new decisions based on new information when presented properly. Customers do not like to look foolish or indecisive, nor do they like to be seen changing their mind as they perceive this indicates weakness and inability to make decisions.

It is important that you do not offend nor contend with your customers over who is right or wrong. If you prove your point that you are right yet lose the customer because he has been embarrassed or shown-up then did you really win?

Was it important that you proved your point and forced the customer to acknowledge you were right? This is where using the fact that customers will make new decisions on new information becomes so important. When you are able to understand the customers question and show him credibility by letting him know that was a great question and good insight while you are using his question to zero in on the answer, then the customer feels justified in making new decisions based on the new information when it is presented professionally. These types of opportunities are best performed by acknowledging the worth of the question and insight of the customer and then asking them if they will consider the new information you are going to share with them as further validation of your product or service.

As with closing techniques, there are hundreds of answers to objections and most closing sequences are interwoven in the objection itself that leads to a specific or particular close. I have earlier related to you that the best way to get rid of objections is to deal with them earlier in your presentation. When you as the salesperson raise the point regarding a common objection and then relate an experience or take action to overcome that objection during that interlude then you are removing that objection from the final closing sequence. As with the 'I want to think about it' objection, by addressing it on my terms early in the presentation, I have removed one obstacle to overcome at the end.

Knowing or becoming familiar with particular objections allows you to build ways to overcome them in your presentation. Nevertheless, objections do often occur at the end of your presentation and close, and I am going to relate the easiest sequence to follow that I have learned through the years. This technique is designed to establish what the core reason is behind the objection – the real reason why the sale is not being finalised.

Many times customers use common delay objections because they do not want to hurt the salesperson's feelings or because they do not really understand everything, so they ask for more time. It is also a proven fact that customers do not want to say 'NO' so they ask for time, say they will think about it, ask for brochures, tell you they will call back, say they were just investigating or just looking, and even that they are not sure they actually want what you are selling. Customers will do any number of things to put off a buying decision while trying to not say 'NO' because they don't want to feel uncomfortable and apply any pressure on themselves.

A small minority of customers actually do come out and say no, and I encourage that, because it leads to final decisions. Once again, initial 'NO's' generally mean 'know' so I do not just stop the process, this is where the professionalism and where elite salespeople earn their reputation.

What these 'no's' say to me is the customer is decisive and able to make up his mind, so if I do my job properly and answer his outstanding questions and handle his objections, then chances are very good he will say yes and finalise the sale.

The most common objections are fairly well known to all, and I will list a few:

1. I want to think about it (I want to talk it over with X, I would like to review the information, I need a bit more time).
2. Price / Cost.
3. Now is not a good time, later I will be more prepared.

Now while there are literally hundreds of variations and the same number of specific replies to all the variations, most objections are some form of the above. Whether the objection relates to time or money, it is usually connected to one of the two or both. Think again of your own buying experiences. If you want something, you will ask the questions and dig for the information because you are serious about it and you want it. You are trying to ensure you are making a good choice, so questions need to be asked. If you are not sure, you will ask for more time.

If you are not sure you can afford it, you will question the price / cost and investigate your own finances to clarify. When you have been in situations where the information was clear, the salesperson was professional and answered your questions and the price was right, what did you do… you finalised the sale, didn't you? However, if the salesperson was not so good and did not answer all your questions, who was the burden left with – you, the customer – you now had to sell to yourself because the salesperson was not doing the job. Because you are courteous, you do not say to the salesperson that they are not doing the job, what you do is ask for time to consider it.

While average salespeople are able to supply limitless excuses as to why the customer did not buy, including the famous "I have done everything to close the sale, and the customer just wants a little time to finalise their choice, I am sure they will be calling back". Or "This is a great prospect; they want me to call back next week to finalise the order". Translation: the fact is that any excuse will do if you, the salesperson, did not do your job, and holding out for those rare occasions when a customer just might call back will ruin your sales career.

These rare occasions tend to cloud perspective and knowing that getting a decision is the 'best' way to operate. What do I mean by this comment, any excuse will do? When you choose to become a true professional you eliminate excuses. You take it upon yourself to work at your profession which means you eliminate mistakes and excuses. If it did not work – why becomes the most important question. Why did it end this way, what could you have done to obtain a different result? Why did the customer say that, why did I say what I said? What are you going to do to better your performance? Desire and effort to study, learn, practice, ask questions, find out what you can do better, how you can become the best – are these qualities you possess?

Example – a neighbour comes to you and asks to borrow your lawnmower. Now you know this neighbour has the knack for destroying all of the equipment you have lent him in the past and you really do not want to lend him your lawnmower. So when he asks you, you say, I'm sorry neighbour, I can't lend you my lawnmower because it is Tuesday and there is a full moon tonight. The neighbor says, "what are you talking about... what has that got to do with me borrowing your lawnmower?" And you say, "it has nothing to do with it, but one excuse is as good as another".

Any excuse will do… if you do not want to do something, you can find a million excuses for not doing it. It does not excuse your action; it just allows you to excuse yourself from doing what you should actually be doing. Excuses are just that, they are excuses for why you did not perform. It does not justify the result; it simply becomes an excuse that perpetuates mediocrity. Enough of that, let's see the formula for objections.

RULE NUMBER ONE FOR OBJECTIONS

'Identify and justify' - you must now ensure that the objection stated is real. The easiest and most professional way to do this is to use the objection as the reason they will buy if the objection is resolved. This is otherwise known as using the reason they will not buy as the reason they will buy. Sound confusing? Maybe, but follow the logic through this example:

◊ (Objection) Price is too high, I cannot afford that.
◊ (Salesperson) Mr. X, that is fair and I want to address the price concern with you… however… please help me understand you properly if you will. IF the price were not an issue. Let's say we are able to resolve the price concern, are you saying then that you would like to take advantage of the product or service? What I am asking is that if the price were not a concern you would like to have the product, yes?

What I am doing here is identifying the real issue. Is it price or is there something else? What I do is isolate the objection to find out if that is really the objection or reason holding them back from buying. If that is really the objection the client will say "yes" to my question. With that I am able to isolate price and move forward with resolving that objection.

That is what is meant by the reason they will not buy is the reason they will buy. Still confused? If I am able to resolve the price issue, then the objection of price becomes the reason I can close the sale if I handle it properly and satisfy the customer's concern. Let's continue with the example:

◊ (Customer) Yes, that's correct.
◊ (Salesperson) Mr. X, just to be sure I understand you, you are saying that if the question of the price can be sorted out, then you will be happy to proceed with the product, correct?
◊ (Customer) yes, that's correct.
◊ (Salesperson) O.K., well let's look at the price issue then shall we? Mr. X, what is the problem you have with the price? After all, we are only able to satisfy you if the product does everything you believe you should be paying for, correct? (rhetorical, don't stop here, just nod your head and get the customer to agree in principle to the context) Mr. X, with all the benefits and features I have showcased for you, and your agreement with me that the product would suit your wants and needs, what price do you feel would be acceptable based on everything our product will do for you… would you feel more comfortable if we removed some of the features and benefits you agreed were so suited to your requirements in order to lower the price? I wouldn't think you would want some of the real attributes of the product to be removed just to offer a bit of a lower price, would you? After all, like they say, it is better to invest in quality then to be penny wise and pound foolish, isn't it Mr. X?… with that in mind, what price would you feel is justified for all the value you are receiving… what price would you put on the product Mr. X?

Now what you are doing is reinforcing the isolation of the objection. If it is really price then the customer will now tell you what price they feel the product is worth. From the questions you posed you will now discover whether the customer is serious about wanting the product or if they are just playing games. If they tell you a ridiculous price you can maintain your professionalism and ask them where they believe they can find this value and quality for the price they are stating. If you know your product market, you will know whether your quality level product is available at ridiculous prices. When or if a customer responds with such a low price, I say:

◊ (Salesperson) Mr. X, I am sure you can relate to this example. When you get good value for a really good product you remember it and tell others what a good product you have. Let's use a refrigerator. You buy a top of the line refrigerator and it gives you great service for years and the features are useful. You are happy to tell others what a good product it is, even though it may have cost a bit more, it was worth it for the value you have received from it. In reverse, you buy the economy refrigerator and constantly require service and in a short time it just is not worth it anymore. You will remember exactly what you paid for that refrigerator wont you? When you tell people about it you will state exactly what you paid for that piece of junk… the worst investment you ever made, useless junk, never again will you buy cheap just to save a few pennies. Mr. X, we believe in superb value for your investment. We want you to talk about us in the future and be happy with the decision you made to invest wisely and we ensure we build quality into everything we do. We learned long ago, rather take a few minutes to explain the price and ensure long lasting quality in our product instead of discount pricing and apologise long term for poor quality in the product. I'm sure you would agree that long lasting quality overcomes cheaper pricing when it means lesser quality, wouldn't you Mr X? So, I just need to ask you Mr X, would you like to take advantage of our product designed to give you years of service and benefits or would you rather pursue lesser quality products and prices?

Remember here, you are dealing with a questionable customer now… they have stated a ridiculous price to you, either trying to low-ball you or force your hand or see if you will crumple under pressure. OR, they are not interested and are just being spiteful. Thus your ending question is a bit pointed because you now need to determine whether they are serious about your product or if you are wasting your time. If customers want to buy junk then let them go buy it, at least you have your decision! Lets say that the customer is serious about your offer and they consider your offer to ask them what they believe is a fair price as a very generous offer.

What they will also do is reflect on other products they know or what they feel is fair. They will then state what they believe is a fair price. And that is what I want them to do. The next step in the objection becoming the reason to buy is to minimise the difference….

◊ (Salesperson) Mr X, that is fair and I appreciate your consideration on what you believe is a fair price. When you consider this price, have you remembered all the added benefits and functionality we include in the product to ensure customer satisfaction?

So Mr X, you are of the belief that $XXX is the price you are happy with and our price is $XXX, therefore the difference is only $XXX. Mr X, let's take a look at what you get for that small difference in price, after all, we are only talking about $X. (what you are doing now is minimising the difference. If they feel $1500 is fair and your price is $2000, the difference is only $500 and this is what you now concentrate on… only the difference in price. After all, they have accepted their own price of $1500, so you are no longer selling that portion of the deal; you are only validating and proving the value of your $500 difference!). (Take a minute to recap a few highlights that were especially attractive to the customer – hone in on extra value items that excited the customer so they can see the value of that small difference, and then move on to this) – Mr. X, in real terms the difference is only $41 per month over just one year… or less that $1.50 per day for all the added value and satisfaction you will receive in the product. I am sure that for such a tiny amount in difference that you would agree the product and price we offer is really designed to satisfy even the most demanding customers, and we do have lots of satisfied customers Mr X, wouldn't you like to be one of them?... how can we take care of this for you Mr. X, cash, check or credit card? (And be quiet!)

If you work through this final segment where you arrive at the difference in price breakdown and the customer is not with you in agreeing with your direction, and you feel you still need a confirmation example to bring home your value point, use the same refrigerator story… it relates the same message of buying quality. Once you relate the refrigerator story, come right back to your final close: "I am sure that for such a tiny amount in difference that you would agree the product and price we offer is really designed to satisfy even the most demanding customers, and we do have lots of satisfied customers Mr X, wouldn't you like to be one of them?… how can we take care of this for you Mr. X, cash, check or credit card? (And be quiet!)".

Let's just take the other famous one – I want to think about it:

◊ (Customer) I really like what you have shown me, can you leave some brochures so I can think about it and I will get back to you.
◊ (Salesperson) Mr. X, that's fair and I appreciate that you want to make the BEST choice when it comes to this decision. As we spoke about a little bit earlier, I am sure you will recall that we agreed that the best time to make the best decision is when the information is fresh and in front of you, and while you have an expert available to answer any questions that you may have. With that in mind, it seems then that I may have missed something or maybe something wasn't absolutely clear for you in order for you to make the best choice now while we are together. I would really appreciate it then if you would please help me out by feeling free to indicate to me if there is something that wasn't clear or a question you may have…

… was it related to what the features are, or the benefits? Or perhaps the choice of offerings or the pricing?? (And be quiet now, let them speak)

◊ (Customer) No nothing really, I understand everything you have said, I just need some time to think / speak to partner / review the offer / go through everything.

◊ (Salesperson) Fair enough Mr X, I can see you are very serious about this and I want you to know that I value your decision very much. So much so that I cannot really leave here with you feeling that the offer or the price is not clear and attractive enough for you to either say yes or no. Mr X, I would not be offended in the least if you feel this is not the right product for you and you need to say 'no'. I would rather you say 'no' than allow me to leave and have me worried that I didn't complete the job I was sent here to do.

Mr X, if I read you correctly, you can see the benefits and the value of the product and what it will do for you, yes?... And with that Mr. X, if you can see the benefits of what the product will do for you, when would you want to take advantage of those benefits?... May I be so kind as to understand from you then, what would be the benefit of waiting? (And be quiet, the customer is going to say something of value here.) (The above scenario is a bit direct, yet you can be subtle and polite and genuine while asking these 'what' related questions. You are trying to find out 'what' is holding him back from deciding.)

What is very compelling here is the fact that it is very hard for customers to find benefits from waiting. You are appealing to their logic and better judgment.

◊ (Salesperson) (Another way to address this is to minimise the "time" issue like you did with price by asking 'when' related questions). Mr. X that is fair, may I ask then; when do you feel would be the best time to make this decision? As we have previously discussed, the 'best' time is when the information is fresh and right in front of you, and when you have an expert in front of you who can answer any questions you might have. Mr. X, when would be a better time than now? (Be quiet, they are going to let you know what to do)

◊ (Customer) Well I don't need long, perhaps just a day or two.
◊ (Salesperson) Mr. X, since I can see you are serious about this, what I am going to do is write up the details for you so you can see exactly what you are working with before I leave… Mr X, which option did you prefer? And which method will be easiest for you to use, the cash, check or credit card?

(And I write it up as a visual benefit to the customer – when I am done, this is what I do next:) Mr X, now that it is clear in front of you, what I am going to do is step out for thirty minutes. I have some calls / errands / admin to take care of and that will give you time to consider the offer. When I get back you may let me know what you would like to do… (And out the door I go – and you must get up and go; it is an action predicated sequence).

This always results in a decision of some sort; either the customer stops you and finalises with you or appreciates you giving them time without you sitting there and will give you a decision when you return.

◊ (Salesperson) (Another way is to get to this point and write up the order and then ask them to do you a favour)… Mr. X, because I have so many people to see and it is almost impossible for me to come back, may I please ask you this favour? Let us complete the order and as a solution to both of us, I will date the order, and you may date the check for three days from now. This will give you time to cancel the order and the check if you feel you are not prepared to take advantage of the offer. I will then tear the order and the check up and confirm cancellation with you immediately. If you are o.k. with your decision to take advantage of the offer then everything is in place and I will confirm with you to process the order and the check and it will save us both a lot of time and effort. Mr X, how does that work out for you? (And be quiet).

The whole point is to use their objection, minimise, isolate, interrogate, question and dig to find out the root of the problem or question. And remember, the quest is to obtain a decision, that is your goal, obviously you want to get a 'yes' decision, but do not lose sight of the fact that the decision is the key objective.

Rule Number One recap – identify and justify the objection is real. You must identify and isolate the objection so you know what you are working with and can answer that specific objection.

If there are a number of misunderstandings or concerns inside there, you must smoke them out. Here is when you have to use what the customer gives you in return… if they say price, your question to them is – "Mr X, if I understand you correctly you are saying price is the only issue, correct?"

Always repeat the objection back to them in question form to ensure you understand it correctly and also to isolate and ensure you are dealing with this ONE objection so you can resolve it and close the sale.

What the objection is becomes the reason they will buy; if it is price and you can answer their question on price, then the sale is made. The objection becomes your closing sequence, so make sure you use it! If the customer says price and you start talking about features, you have missed the objection and the objection is going to come back again or the customer is going to realise you are not listening to him and they are going to tell you they want to think about it and leave… no sale, no decision.

Do not ignore the objection – use it and find out if it is real. If it is not real, they will tell you what is real. If you say "Mr X, if I understand you correctly you are saying price is the only issue, correct?" and they say… well actually I am not sure I will use the product… then price is not the objection, they are not sold on the product!

And at this point you need to investigate that concern – "Mr X, so that I understand you correctly, you are not sure you will use the product; will you be a bit more detailed for me so I understand please?" – ask and you will find out, don't ask and you are shooting in the dark hoping to hit a moving target.

Finding the true objection is like diagnosing an illness. What does the doctor do, ask questions, ask what symptoms, how long, history of the illness, tests are done, exams, etc. All the investigations done by the doctor are done to isolate the illness so it can be treated and cured. Imagine you go in with malaria and instead of asking you questions to investigate where you were or what you have been in contact with, the doctor just assumes it is flu and prescribes some medicine to take and off you go.

You could die or get worse or permanently cause yourself damage because the wrong diagnosis was made and no effort taken to investigate and find the cause. You have to do the same thing. Don't be afraid of the objection – use it, it is the symptom in your case; you must ask the right questions to diagnose the cause and then treat it with the right cure!

RULE NUMBER TWO

"If – Then" – This is a simple method that is easy to remember and becomes a rule for nearly everything you do in sales, especially in overcoming objections. The theory and concept is basic, 'If' I do this, 'Then' you will do that. 'If' I ask you to do this, 'Then' I will do this in return. It is like a see-saw, if one end goes up, the other end comes down. For every action there is a reaction, and closing while overcoming objections is the same principle. It is a principle that helps customers feel secure in the fact that you are in this together; that the commitments and actions are not solely the responsibility of the customer. Customers appreciate it when they know that you are also making commitments and taking responsibility for activities required in the sale.

Example – "Mr. X, if we can ask you to do this, then this is what we are going to do for you". "Mr. X, if we do this for you, then we will appreciate that you do this for us".

Too often salespeople who lack in confidence feel they must do everything, say everything, and take ownership of all facets of the sales process. These salespeople never ask customers to make any commitments or confirmations, and they fail to ask the customer to take action. They remove the customer from the equation and never require the customer to participate, nor especially make commitments or confirmations. When the sales person gets to the end of his presentation, if they should be so bold as to ask for a decision, the customer is shocked and stunned.

This is when they retreat into their shell, because how can they make a commitment now when they have been a bystander and 'view-only' window shopper just minutes before? These situations are far too familiar to me and I have seen way too many salespeople get to the end and then quite simply fade away. Salespeople commit to what they will do for the customer, what they will give them – pricing concessions, special rates, etc. – in an effort to show how willing they are to make the customer happy. What they fail to do is ever ask the customer what the customer will give in return if the salesperson makes all these concessions and compromises.

The sales process is a dance, a partnership. And like any dance, 'If' the lead partner steps forward, 'Then' the led partner takes a step backwards. It is an action orientated participation and most importantly a participation of both parties.

Whatever the lead partner does (the 'If' part of the dance), the led partner reciprocates or reacts to the action (the 'Then' part of the dance). So please remember, a partnership takes more than one person and the "If – Then" process requires participation from both the presenter and the customer. It is not a one way street or one way recital; the customer has just as much responsibility to participate as you do and you need their buy-in, their agreement, and their confirmations and commitments. Build as many "If – Then" scenarios into your close as possible and prepare for possible objections to come by raising "If – Then" requests to the customer throughout the presentation.

Examples:
◊ If you had this feature in the product, Mr. X, then I'm sure you can see what the benefits are that you receive from that, yes?
◊ If you could name your favourite features in the product Mr X, then what would you say is most important to you?
◊ If we can resolve your question regarding X, then I'm sure you would be happy to proceed, yes Mr. X?
◊ If we do this for you Mr. X, then we will ask this in exchange from you, and that's fair isn't it?

Recap: "If – Then" is a most useful participation tool to interactively involve customers in the thought making process. Commitments and confirmations from the customer allow the customer to participate and feel useful during the presentation and close.

Without "If – Then" you could find yourself troubled regarding what to say in order to illicit a commitment or confirmation from the customer at crucial times in the process.

RULE NUMBER THREE

Ask and Ye Shall Receive – Ask the customer what they mean by 'NO'. Do they mean no, they do not like the product? Do they mean they do not like something about the way the offer is structured? Do they mean they do not like the price? Do they mean they do not think they will use it? Do they mean they do not understand; they do not have clarity?

If you ask the customer to clarify or help you to understand, he will. If you ask for help or assistance, they will help. If you ask them to explain whatever it is that they might be talking about, they will tell you. Be polite and sincere and genuine about what you are asking them to confirm. Ask them if they like the product. Ask them if they can see themselves using it and receiving the benefits. Ask them to help you understand their point or issue.

The more you ask the more you receive… answers, commitments, confirmations, facts, details, yes replies, buying replies, etc. Be fair and let them make their statement, then ask if you have understood it correctly before answering. It becomes important for you to confirm their objection, and then proceed with helping to resolve it – thus eliminating the objection from being a sale stopper and more often establishing that objection issue as a main reason to purchase the product.

Of course, just like with "IF – Then", the opposite is also true. Ask nothing and get nothing in return. If you accept the objection as a deal breaker and do not seek to establish the validity, then you have accepted a 'NO' sale without even asking why. Never be insecure about asking questions. Customers respect the fact that you are caring and interested in their requirements, so listen…

RULE NUMBER FOUR

Minimise – Establish ways to minimise less than perfect fits. There is hardly a product on the planet that does absolutely 100% of what each customer wants. Regardless of how clever and creative and how feature rich and full of functionality the product may be, there is always room for improvement. There is always a need to improve, enhance, grow, develop, change, and continuously re-invent the products we use every day. Just notice how even the major brands come up with 'new & improved' enhancements.

Even the most efficient and effective products that we love to brag about could stand for ever so slight improvements, isn't that so? Ever hear the routing that goes something like: "Wow, this is a really useful product. It can do so many things and it is so handy… but… if it only had this one other thing. Or if it could just do this little bit more, if it were just a bit faster a bit easier," etc. Ever hear those statements or say those statements?

Your product and customer perception is the same story. Customers will often object at the end by saying, if the product only did this, or that. If it only had this one extra feature. If it was only a tad less expensive. If I had only been better prepared. If the timing was just a little better…

Once again, you can begin by acknowledging and understanding their concerns and their questions. Ask them the objection in your words to ensure you both understand the same thing and while using the objection as the reason they will buy, you can often minimise the objection or the request by upholding other key strong features and benefits of the product.

(Salesperson) – Mr. X, I realise that this particular feature request is important to you; would you say it is more important than XXX or less important to you than XXX? The reason I am asking is that, like with any product designed to cover so many key elements and provide such broad functionality, it becomes nearly impossible to satisfy every single request that may arise. If we did that, the product would never be released (smile); we would spend all our time continually adding and enhancing and never allowing customers to benefit from the so many features that actually do exist already.

I'm sure you would agree Mr. X, some items are absolutely critical, and some are nice to have. When it comes to your needs and wants, we have spent time to ensure that X, Y, Z are more than accounted for and actually exactly what you have been looking for, so Mr. X, in light of these many overwhelming features that are what you require, how important is X? Maybe it is minimised when surrounded by all the functionality that the product does have, which is what you want isn't it Mr. X?

(Salesperson) – (You may also re-highlight the many benefits and qualities of the product by saying:) We try very hard to ensure we incorporate as many features as humanly possible to ensure our many customers remain satisfied and happy with their decision. In doing this, we must maintain very high standards while providing the very best product for the very best price. You see, we could have put even more into the product, but that would take more time, longer release cycles, and higher prices to cover for all the additional R&D and development time.

We felt it best to offer this huge stack of features and benefits for this small amount of money as opposed to an even bigger stack of features, but for a much higher price tag, thus reducing the number of customers who can benefit from such a product to relatively few instead of many. Mr. X, we want you to get the very best for your investment and I am sure you would agree that the amount of features and benefits we have built into the product far outweighs the price and the one or two minor developments that would result in delays and higher prices... yes Mr. X?

To finalise on the 'minimise' aspect – Most objections are minor attempts to gain time or make excuses for delaying decisions. If you are able to minimise the effects of price difference, missing features, time restraints, concerns of almost any type, then you will be able to focus the customer on the benefits of making a 'yes' decision as opposed to being consumed with minor aspects that are clouding the main prize... a product or service that will work for the customer.

Minimising also allows the customer to unveil what really is important and what is not. Until this time, all objections may look the same, but when you ask the customer what is most important, you start to get to the heart of the matter and you are able to see what is actually important to the customer in the end. If you minimise a feature or objection and the customer says to you, that is really a major issue for him, then you are able to address that (Use Rule #1).

The conclusion of the 'Overcoming Objections' chapter is to emphasise the fact that objections are your friends. They are the reason customers will buy if you do your job properly. Just like with all aspects of the process, take your time, ask the right questions, be genuine and look for the "win-win" in the process.

Customers are just as anxious to own a product or service that does something for them that they benefit from as you are to make a sale and extract your portion of commission. When you sincerely ask them what they mean, and could they please explain, and would they mind detailing for you exactly what they are looking for, you will unlock the opportunities to close many more sales.

Customers are our partners in this process; it takes both of us, in unison. If you take action and step on their toes because you are not leading them properly, they are going to get frustrated and upset. These are often the pushy salesperson that just keeps pushing for a sale, not concerned if you get your toes stepped on in the process, as long as they get the result – a sale. These are not professionals, they are bullies.

The objection process is the same dance, lead and respond, ask and receive, support and balance, once you understand that objections do not need to be avoided the sooner you can manage them and improve your "yes" percentage. And remember, the more you can build known objections into your sales process, the easier it is for both of you to arrive at the conclusion on the same page and with very few unanswered questions. This is without a doubt the most professional way to go.

I have only highlighted a few examples or rules in this section because I believe these four simple methods can successfully help you overcome more than 90% of the objections of today. There is no need to procrastinate and wait until you learn the exact right answer to every single objection known.

It is more important to learn and apply a few solid rules and use them as templates and examples for nearly every objection you will come across. And pay attention… customers will alert you to gaps in your presentation or process through objections. If you are attentive, you will notice them and then set about to fix them in your presentation. If you are not attentive you will continue to hear them over and over until it finally does sink in or you are overcome by the objection that wouldn't die… you choose!

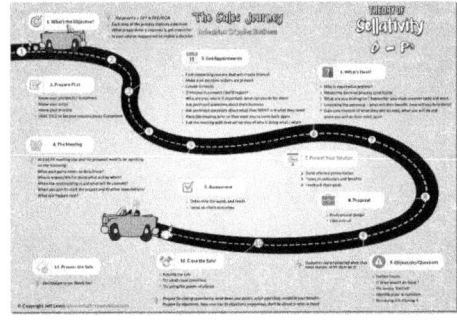

Get your beautiful FREE bonus
"Sales Journey Wall Chart"

Visit
www.sellativitysolutions.com

CHAPTER ELEVEN

Conclusion

As the book draws to a close, the process is the most important aspect of the learning experience. Take the time to be a professional and learn the 'best' way. Then, just like the unconsciously competent of the professional world, selling becomes part of what you do and what you are. You do not have to contemplate every single action, you simply apply the tried and proven methods you have learned and practiced a hundred times. Just like that surgeon, you know your procedure and process, you follow the plan and achieve the results.

I want to leave with you one final section which will compile the extraordinary journey I have taken to lead me to this "Theory of Sellativity". This simple life lessons reminder list, captures some key aspects of what makes a rewarding and engaging life. If you follow these seven Life Lessons, you will not only be a happier person – you will be a terrific and successful sales processional.

Life Lessons:

1. **Love what you do** – if you are going to sell, be passionate about it. You cannot spend your life doing something you are not passionate about. If you do, it will suck the life out of you and leave you dry and empty.
2. **Enjoy every day** – every day is a new adventure. New opportunities present themselves every single day. If it is not happening for you, then it is your fault because you are responsible for your actions. Perhaps you are not paying attention to the signs and clues and opportunities that are there everyday? The opportunities are there – are you?
3. **Invest yourself into this project or whatever project you have in mind** – it is not hard to learn nor hard to do, but it does involve investment of yourself and your time and your dedication and practice to get it right.

4.   **Love your life, Live your life and Choose your life** – Love what you do and the opportunities you will encounter; they are the spice of life and create the soul of your personality. Live your life; don't let life dictate what will become of you and what your life will be today… you must live your life – and you must make your choices. No-one can choose for you, no matter what the circumstance, you still have the ability to choose how you deal with it. Your decisions and your actions determine what results you will achieve.

5.   **No excuses** – Zig Ziglar used to say "any excuse will do – pick one… one is as good as another if you want an excuse". All this means is that you take responsibility for your actions and results. If you are not achieving the results you expect, don't look for excuses – look for solutions.

6.   **Don't plan to get around to it** – get to it! Another Zig-ism is when he hands out round disks and has written on it : round tuit. And then he explains that most people say they will do it when they get around to it… so now you have a 'round tuit', it's in your hand, so you have your round tuit, so get to it!

7. **Be true to yourself.** Be professional and apply the golden rule – or my version of the golden rule: you reap what you sow. You cannot be one type of person and another type of salesperson – your true colors will shine through. This to me is just plain common sense – you can't plant corn and get beans. You cannot treat people with contempt or disparage them and expect good things in return. You cannot con someone and take advantage of them and expect not to be taken advantage of in return. You get what you give in this business and I have learned that when you give professional assistance and service, you get professional responses and reciprocation. You also only get as good in this business as you give in preparation. If you invest good effort in preparation, you receive a good crop in return. When you give of yourself, you get returns which are equivalent.

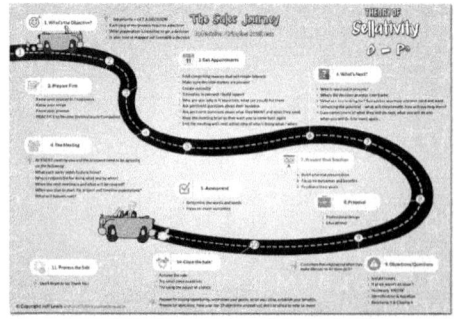

Get your beautiful FREE bonus
"Sales Journey Wall Chart"

Visit
www.sellativitysolutions.com

Index

A
About Jeff Lewis xi
ACTION 161

C
CLOSE NUMBER ONE 163
CLOSE NUMBER THREE 172
CLOSE NUMBER TWO 170
Closing Technique 153
Closing the Sale 129
Conclusion 203

D
Daryl Blundell ix

E
Endorsements vii

F
FEATURES AND BENEFITS 120
FIRST IMPRESSIONS 81
Foreword v

G
Getting a Decision 87

I
Introduction xxi

L
LIFE LESSON 42

N
NEEDS VS. WANTS 123

O
Objective 41
OPENING - THE FIRST THREE MINUTES 82
Overcoming Objections 177

P
Peter Whalley vii
Preparation 53
PREPARATION as noun 71
Process 69
PROCESS PREPARATION 72

R
Real Life Experience xvii
RULE NUMBER FOUR 197
RULE NUMBER ONE FOR OBJECTIONS 183
RULE NUMBER THREE 196
RULE NUMBER TWO 193

S
Selling Points 119
STORY STORY STORY 125

T
The ASSUMPTIVE ACTION CHOICE 157
The formula 41
The Secret Revealed vii
The Story Behind the Story 27
The Theory of Sellativity 37

U
Unconsciously Incompetent 113

www.ingramcontent.com/pod-product-compliance
Lightning Source LLC
Chambersburg PA
CBHW051905170526
45168CB00001B/258